O·F·F·I·C·E AUTOMATION

JEKYLL OR HYDE?

HIGHLIGHTS OF THE INTERNATIONAL CONFERENCE ON OFFICE WORK & NEW TECHNOLOGY ■ EDITED BY DANIEL MARSCHALL AND JUDITH GREGORY

WORKING WOMEN EDUCATION FUND

Cover design by Al Wasco

ISBN 0-912663-00-6
Library of Congress Catalog Number 83-060764

First Printing, May 1983

Working Women Education Fund
1224 Huron Road
Cleveland, Ohio 44115

Contents

III.   Effects on the Quality and Organization of Work

IV. Occupational Health and the Computerized Office

V. Future Directions for Industry, Labor and Public Policy

Acknowledgments

The editors and the Working Woman Education Fund are grateful to the German Marshall Fund of the United States for its generous support of both the International Conference on Office Work and New Technology and the publication of this book.

We would also like to thank the Youth Project for its support of the conference, and Joel Makower of Tilden Press for his assistance in the production of this book. We are grateful to Jane Fleishman, Christina Graf, Sarah Kuhn, Beatriz Manz, and the staff and members of 9 to 5 who provided invaluable assistance at the conference.

Unfortunately, we are not able to include all of the presentations from the conference in this volume. We are indebted to the following conference speakers whose contributions were vital to this unique gathering:

Paul Adler, "Developments in Policies & Research in France," Harvard Business School, and Dept. of Economics, Barnard College

Sandra Albrecht, "Potentials and Problems of Office Homework," Sociology Department, University of Kansas,

Lawrence Wies Arts, "Impact of Office Automation on Skills & Career Mobility," Department of Social Research, University of Leyden, Netherlands

Dennis Chamot, "Policy Alternatives: Labor, Government and Management Approaches," Assistant Director, Department for Professional Employees, AFL-CIO

Matthew Drennan, "Skills, Education and Training to Prepare for the Automated Office," Graduate School of Public Administration, New York University

Odd Heldre, "Ergonomics and the Computer Industry," President, Tandberg Data Inc., Oslo, Norway

Laura C. Johnson, "Potentials and Problems of Office Homework," Social Planning Council of Metropolitian Toronto, and University of Toronto

George Kohl, "The Redesign of Computerized Work," Research Specialist, Communications Workers of America (CWA)-AFL-CIO

Linda Lampkin, "Effects of New Technologies on Productivity in the Service Industries," Director of Research, American Federation of State, County and Municipal Employees (AFSCME-AFL-CIO)

Pat McDermott, "Alternative Strategies to Address Office Automation," Ontario Labor Relations Board, Toronto

Heather Menzies, "Impact of Office Automation on Skills & Career Mobility," Author, *Women & the Chip* and *Computers and Your Job*, Ottawa

Debra Ness, "Skills, Education and Training to Prepare for the Automated Office," Career Development, Service Employees International Union (SEIU)-AFL-CIO, CLC

Margrethe Olson, "Potentials and Problems of Office Homework," CAIS, Graduate School of Business Administration, New York University

Ratna Ray, "Employment Impacts: State of the Research," Technology for People and Women's Bureau, Labour Canada, Ottawa

Elio R. Rotolo, "Office Automation: Company Experiences," Vice President, Industrial Engineering, Security Pacific National Bank

Jon B. Ryberg, "Office Automation: Company Experiences," Facility Management Institute, Division of Herman Miller Research Corp.

Julia Stallibrass, "Effects of Technical Change on White Collar Workers in the Public Sector of Britain," National and Local Government Officers Association (NALGO), London, Great Britain

Lawrence Tesler, "Choices in Designing Computer Systems," Personal Office System Division, Apple Computer Inc.

Joan Tighe, "Job Stress, Job Design and Work Organization," Policy Training Center, Boston

Diane Wernecke, "Employment Impacts: State of the Research," Research Consultant, International Labor Office

Connie Winkler, "Occupational Trends in Computer-Related Jobs," Consultant, and former editor, *Computer Career News*, New York

Amy Wohl, "Technologies of the 1980s: Telecommunications & Office Automation," President, Advanced Office Concepts, Bala Cynwyd, PA

Introduction

In 1980, the Working Women Education Fund and 9 to 5, the National Association of Working Women, published **Race Against Time: Automation of the Office**. This publication was the first statement on office automation from the viewpoint of United States office workers themselves.

Race Against Time was something of a cry in the wilderness. The office workers' daily problems with automation had been strangely invisible. Our publication broke the silence, calling attention to such problems as the muscle strain resulting from poorly designed equipment, the monotony and stress accompanying certain machine-paced jobs, the decline of pay and career opportunity for employees in certain automated offices. To us, these problems arising from office automation were of the utmost urgency. **Race Against Time** provided a popular framework for discussing them.

And **Race Against Time** sounded an alarm. In it, we warned that automation was ushering in an epidemic of stress-related diseases among office workers; that far from creating exciting job opportunities, automation was eliminating and de-skilling many good clerical jobs; and that many of the new jobs created by automation were more monotonous and tedious than ever before.

A national debate began. The office of the future could be a pleasant and productive place to work, or it could be a disaster area, replete with health hazards, low morale, low pay, low productivity, and massive job loss. The outcome depended on specific decisions that would be made in this decade.

The debate moved to a new stage in October, 1982, in Boston, Massachusetts, when the Working Women Education Fund and 9 to 5 sponsored the International Conference on Office Work and New Technology. The 350 participants—twenty-five of them from European countries and Canada—included representatives of every constituency and discussion of every facet of office automation. Exchanging views in workshops and panel discussions were representatives of the computer industry, the corporate sector, public policy makers, trade unionists, researchers, computer skills instructors, occupational health experts, sociologists, professors, and individual office workers.

It was the firm consensus of the conference participants that there are indeed problems in the way automation is being used in the modern office—problems with job design, job loss, and health and safety.

But more important, the conference moved the consensus one step further still. It established that there are solutions to the problems. Viable alternatives in the use of new technology do exist and have been successfully put into action. Of this, our European colleagues presented ample proof. They detailed their practical experience in implementing office automation in ways that maximized job satisfaction, exciting career paths, and positive social interaction in the office, without sacrificing efficiency. From their presentations, American participants gained a new understanding of the choices facing all of us as we shape the office of the future.

Automation of the office is not yet accomplished fact. The opportunity is before us to identify the problems and solve them. We can learn from the European experience and create office systems that are productive and cost-effective while paying greater attention to the human factors.

I hope that **Office Automation: Jekyll or Hyde** will further our understanding of the task before us and encourage us all to take action for a positive future.

Karen Nussbaum
Executive Director
9 to 5, National Association of Working Women
President, District 925
Service Employees International Union
Cleveland, April, 1983

I. The Big Picture

Choices in the Development of Office Automation

Harley Shaiken
Program in Science, Technology & Society
Massachusetts Institute of Technology

I am very pleased to give the opening remarks at this important conference. It culminates several years of work by 9 to5 and the Working Women Education Fund in the area of office automation—far before it was the glamorous issue it has become today. I think this work is central and has been central in raising the issue of automation in a constructive way for the entire society.

Today the issue is more critical than ever. Factories and offices in the United States are going through a period of rapid and pervasive technological change. The unasked question is: how do we evaluate the extraordinary transformations taking place around us?

In the February 1982 issue of **Science** magazine, the president-elect of the American Association for the Advancement of Science, Anna J. Harrison, laid out three premises for looking at technological change: "First, every technological innovation, regardless of how great its *positive* impact on society, also has a *negative* impact. Second, the benefits and the negative impacts may be experienced by *different* subsets of society. And finally, the benefits and the negative impacts may be experienced in *different* time-frames." (Emphasis added.)

As a society, are we considering office automation today from the balanced perspective that Professor Harrison lays out, or are the social costs being buried to speed the diffusion of automation at any price? Unfortunately, I think the latter may be the case.

In fact there are two additional questions that we ought to be asking. What are the alternatives? And how are the decisions made? The question of alternatives is at the core of this gathering. The conference structure seeks to do more than explore the impact of automation on the office. Impact implies after-the-fact and that really is too narrow a focus. We should go beyond assuming the inevitability of technological change to speak about the nature and character of that change. More importantly, we should also look at the ways technology itself can be shaped to avoid the negative consequences that increasingly are present.

To discuss alternatives, we must carefully examine issues of design, the rate of deployment, and the use of the technology. These decisions are the product of human beings. They don't inevitably spring forth from the nature of micro-processors or computers. And because they are human decisions, they deserve the broadest possible public scrutiny and examination. This conference represents an important step in that process.

In fact, this program is unique because it brings together a wide range of participants with both practical and theoretical experience of grappling with these issues. The experience of our European friends and colleagues, in particular, is pivotal, for the social questions surrounding office automation have been raised earlier and more sharply in many European countries. Of course, our European friends are not bringing us blueprints for change. Instead, they are contributing valuable insights, ideas, strategies and experiences that we in the United States must mold and adapt to the realities that we face today.

The second additional question we should be asking is: How are the decisions made? That is, who decides and on what basis? Today, issues of technological change are exclusively managerial decisions, and the central driver of change is return on investment. Last week, while writing an opinion-editorial piece in the **New York Times,** William Agee, Chairman of Bendix, who is also known as a Detroit-based merger and acquisition specialist, wrote that "the foremost objective of responsible management is improving the value of the shareholders' investment over the long term". But given the scope and the rapidity of technological change today, is this criteria enough to insure a responsible use of the technology for the workers involved and for the larger society? I think not. The well-being of the people who are affected, and the well-being of the community should be the central drivers of technological change. The only way to insure that these concerns are even raised is to integrate the participation of those who are most clearly affected into the basis decisions that govern change.

So it's not a question of whether automation in the abstract means progress; it's really a question of progress for whom and progress towards what goals? These issues are becoming ever more difficult to deal with in the current economic climate. Office automation is a capital intensive technology that is being introduced during a period of economic collapse and what may be long-term economic stagnation. The economic crisis creates enormous pressures to maximize short-term return on investment in new technology, regardless of the long-term social costs. In fact, these economic pressures exacerbate the negative effects of the technology. Nonetheless, it is imperative that we begin grappling with these critical issues. Because the technology is being developed and deployed so rapidly, this conference is more urgent today that it would have been even a year ago.

Myths about the Electronic Office

Several years ago, 9 to 5 issued a pamphlet, **Race Against Time,** which in my view is one of the most compelling and well thought out statements available on automation in the office. That race against time has become even pressing, yet our ability to develop office automation in a human direction is obscured by three prevalent myths. The mere mention of the term automation seems to conjure up these myths:

- Office automation is always more productive.
- It improves the quality of life on the job under all circumstances.
- The employment impacts will take care of themselves.

As in all folktales, there is a certain amount of truth is each of these three statements. But they obscure more than they reveal. They imply that the potential benefits of the technology will be realized automatically and that the social costs are non-existent.

Before examining these more closely, let's locate office automation in a larger technological context. Office automation is part of a wider computerization of the workplace, based on computers and micro-electronics. This computerization encompasses virtually every productive activity in the U.S. economy, from robots in the Chrysler East Jefferson plant in Detroit to word processors at John Hancock Insurance in Boston. Given the pervasiveness and power of the technology, super-automation is an appropriate term to describe it. This term would also avoid confusing automation based on computers with its more modest cousin of several decades ago.

Today, we are only at the beginning of super-automation's introduction. General Electric tells us that the market for factory automation will rise from $4 billion a year in 1981, to $29 billion a year in 1990. Predicast, a Cleveland consulting firm, tells us that the market for office automation could be $19 billion a year by 1995. Dataquest, another consulting firm, predicts that the market for all electronic office equipment could grow by 34% a year through 1986. Word processors alone will likely become a $6 billion a year industry by 1986, up from a little over $2 billion a year in 1981.

The machines themselves—the word processors and electronic files—are, of course, impressive. But, the most significant development is the way they tie together into an integrated electronic office. And in this context the three myths are worth exploring.

Let's look at the first myth, that office automation is always more productive. The word productivity is used a lot in connection with automation. Virtually everything is done in the name of productivity. Seemingly precise statistics are used to justify all manner of change and when these numbers are run through a computer they become even more precise and appear scientifically mandated.

But productivity is a very difficult concept to accurately define. On the level of the firm, it's usually considered an output for a given input. In a factory producing toasters it's easily measurable. One way is to divide the number of toasters produced by the number of hours it took to produce them. But in the office it's far more difficult to measure productivity because the "product" is the processing of information and the provision of services. These are intangible things. They may or may not relate to the number of memos written, the number of calls answered, files retrieved, or documents typed.

In other words, if an office doubles the number of memos written, it's not necessarily twice as productive. The flow of paper might even be counterproductive. Yet frequently this is precisely the measure that is used to extol the benefits of office automation. And it's not hard to understand why: you can quantify the number of sheets that are produced. Very often you cannot quantify the quality of the service that's being provided.

But this desire for quantification, especially in a precarious economic environment, also creates a drive to deploy systems in a way that pace and monitor the workers involved. Under these circumstances, the improvements in quantity are paid for with a decrease in quality— working relationships are destroyed, the caliber of the service declines, and errors soar. And yet, the end product is referred to as more productive!

Whether or not the restructuring of the office is beneficial requires a better perspective as to what productivity is all about. There is an enormous difference between efficiency and effectiveness. Efficiency is really a measure of the output. Effectiveness is whether or not the office meets the purposes that it is meant to accomplish.

Beyond this, however, the quality of life on the job should be considered a vital part of productivity. In some cases, one approach to office automation may increase output by 3%, let's say, over another approach. But is this the direction in which we should be going if that 3% gain results in a 50% erosion in the quality of life on the job? These considerations seldom, if ever, are brought into the discussion of productivity, yet they should be at the core of that discussion.

Extending Managerial Control
Over the Workplace

Let's look at the second myth, that automation always increases the quality of life on the job. The potential is certainly there. Yet it is ironic that a technology such as word processing, which theoretically requires more skills than the typewriter it replaces, can be used in a way that *de-skills* the secretary or typist; used in a way that increases the monitoring or control and decreases the independence of the worker involved.

A case that appeared in 1982, in **The Journal of Occupational Psychology** illustrates one way that new technology can affect life of the job. The case looks at the introduction of office automation in an engineering consulting firm. The two authors conclude: "Interviews with typists indicated that the change from copy typing to word processing had reduced task variety, meaning and contribution, control over work scheduling and boundary tasks, feedback of results, involvement in preparation and auxiliary tasks, and communication with authors." Removing some of the academic jargon: things didn't look very good in that office.

Other studies done in the U.S. draw similar conclusions. The now famous study by NIOSH (the National Institute of Occupational Safety and Health) of Blue Shield workers in San Francisco in 1979 came to the alarming conclusion the the clerical workers who were studied using VDTs exhibited the highest degree of stress for any occupation that NIOSH had looked at, including air traffic controllers.

In order to understand how office automation results in boring, repetitive, stressful, and controlled work, we have to step back from the machines and systems themselves. These qualities don't flow out of any innate properties of micro-processors, computers or word processors. An authoritarian work environment reflects the goals that inform the design of those systems. And the price is not only job satisfaction, but very often the effectiveness of the office itself.

A west coast consulting firm, in a report on office automation, stated one central managerial goal that has become all too prevalent. I won't mention the name of the consulting firm, because it might embarass the Stanford Research Institute. The goal: "Management has also found with word processing it can for the first time monitor the productivity of secretarial workers and thus gain some degree of control over this clerical function." This theme is repeated by a large producer of word processors. The firm advertises its product in the following way: "A built in reporting system helps you monitor your work flow." And I take it that "you" isn't the secretary or typist involved. "It automatically gives the author's and the typist's name, the document number, the date and time of origin and last revision, required editing time, and the length of the document".

With these design goals in mind, systems are set up for the ease of supervising workers rather than for maximum effectiveness. Machines are designed and deployed in a way where the central goal becomes monitoring and pacing of the job, rather than increasing the autonomy and independence of the worker. There's a hidden but very real cost to moving in this direction. Those systems that pace the job very often "build out" those uniquely human capabilities of skill, initiative, creativity and enthusiasm.

Moreover, a further product of this kind of office is an erosion of skill and control on the job, accompanied by further polarization of the workforce in the society. The end result may be a small number of highly skilled jobs, and a much larger number of de-skilled and less desirable jobs.

These conclusions were echoed by David Rockefeller, a former chairman of the Chase Manhattan Bank. In a recent address to the Detroit Economic Club, he predicted that present forms of automation could lead to: "A two tier society, with satisfying and well-rewarded work for some while the rest are left to grapple for unskilled jobs".

Job Displacement or Growth?

The third myth is that employment will take care of itself. In a recent article in **Datamation,** Paul Strassman of Xerox Corp. even went a step further than this. He predicted that office automation by the turn of the century would create 20 million additional jobs. Now if the problem of technology and employment were as simple as that, we could easily solve our unemployment problems today by rapidly introducing billions of dollars of automated equipment!

But it's not quite that simple. Technology is being introduced today against a background of stagnant economic growth. It's an unprecedented situation. Traditionally, when automation has been introduced, the economy itself was growing, so the same number of workers in a given industry could produce more and more and the society would benefit. But in a slow-growing economy, the result of automation could very well be the same total product produced by fewer and fewer workers. In fact, with a 10% unemployment rate in the United States today, the real issue isn't how many workers will be displaced, but how many workers who are currently on the street will ever return to the jobs they held formerly, or obtain other jobs in the society.

Of course, new technologies do create new jobs. Entire new industries are created. But that's not the issue. The real issue is how many jobs will be created compared to the number that are eliminated? And just as important, in what time-frame will they be created, and where will they be created? Employment in the banking industry, for example, is still growing, although less slowly than it has grown traditionally. Between 1960 and 1973, it grew by 4.5% annually. Between 1973 and 1976, it grew by 3.2%. But today we are seeing the very rapid introduction of new technologies in banking. So one bank in St. Louis recently reported that a new computer system enabled it to handle 35,000 transactions a day more than it had previously handled, with 10% fewer tellers.

Even if employment continues to grow modestly in areas such as insurance and banking, will it be enough to absorb the number of people who are displaced by robots and other forms of automation in the factory? The result may be an "economic vise"—computer automation in the factory pushing people out of traditional manufacturing jobs, and computer automation in the office preventing the creation of the number of jobs that are needed. Employment could be severely squeezed.

Meanwhile, the current shocks thoughout the economy are rewriting our understanding of those occupations traditionally associated with employment growth. Take computer programmers, an occupation frequently promoted as certain to expand in the future. The Bureau of

Labor Statistics has predicted a shortage of 25,000 computer programmers annually in the next ten years. But now we find a surplus of entry level computer programmers. Yes, there is still a shortage of people with 5-10 years of experience. But many people, displaced from a variety of other occupations, had the same idea as to where the opportunities are: become a computer programmer. The result is a surplus that may not go away soon. In 1981, for example, 31,000 people took courses to become computer programmers, compared to half that number in 1978.

Automation does not have to translate into unemployment. But, to avoid major job loss requires a healthy economy and policies targeted to create employment. One example is linking the use of more automation to less work time. The problem will not solve itself.

Power Relations and Systems Design

What then are our choices? We have to go beyond merely posing the question of: "Do we want office automation or are we opposed to automation?" The real issue is what kind of automation we want, and what process is necessary to insure that technological change benefits both the employees involved and the entire society? These problems require more than enlightenment to solve. At issue are questions of power and control as well. Conventional wisdom, for example, tells us roadblocks to automation are really just problems of communication, and users should be involved in the design and implementation of systems. But frequently, this participation merely means user cooperation in installing something that has already been designed with purposes in mind that undermine the user's position.

In other cases, sophisticated managements are increasingly pointing to user participation as undesirable if relations of power are changed, which is often the case. In a recent study, Lynne Marcus of the Sloan School at MIT concludes: "If users are given a genuine opportunity to participate, they will try to change the proposed designs in ways which meet their needs to the exclusion of others. These attempts can lead to a failure of managers and systems analysts to achieve their political objectives".

For those who are affected by change, this is hardly enough. Ultimately, technology is not just a question of machines and systems, but of power and how this power is allocated. We need to better articulate the technical alternatives available. And, at the top of the agenda should be a discussion of the process by which decisions are made. The people who will have to use and live with these technologies should have a say in determining the goals of the system as well as how the system is implemented. A human use of new technology requires a democratic development of that technology as well.

If the social cost of technological change is ignored, it does not go away. In fact the social cost becomes more difficult to pay if it is addressed after the damage is done. In looking at our options, I believe this conference is an exciting and significant first step.

Office Automation: Jekyll or Hyde?

Karen Nussbaum
9 to 5, National Association of Working Women
District 925/Service Employees International Union

This international conference is an historic event. We have brought together leading thinkers and practitioners from around the world, representing every viewpoint—management, computer manufacturers, policy makers, academics, labor and unorganized office workers—to discuss the impact of the revolution in the office.

And the session this noon is unique. Never before have I spoken to a room filled half with office workers, and half with experts and management, and I can think of few other situations where anyone else has.

The message is the same to all of us: we are participating, like it or not, in a dramatic change. The decisions made about office automation over the next few years will determine our futures in profound ways.

In preparation for this conference I went to Europe this summer. I met with a number of experts on automation, several of whom are here today.

The first day I arrived in Denmark, the big news was a study that had been released that day in the United States. The study, conducted by a professor at the University of Pennsylvania, measured the quality of life for 107 nations. This study looked not only at income, but also took into account factors such as infant mortality, adult literacy, health and welfare, political participation, and women's rights. A real measure of the quality of life.

This is the kind of report where the U.S. always comes out first. If not first, then it is big news that Sweden has pushed the U.S. to second place.

Any guesses here how the U.S. ranked? Forty-second. Out of 107 nations, the U.S. was 42nd in quality of life. The Soviet Union was 43rd. Out of 24 rich nations, the U.S. came in 22. 22 out of 24. The reason it was such big news in Denmark is that Denmark came in first.

The U.S. is highly developed technologically, and European nations will often look to the U.S. for technological innovations. But we are underdeveloped in what the technologists call "the human factors."

That is the importance of this conference. As American managers and manufacturers race ahead to automate the office, little time is spent considering the problems, and solutions are considered Pie in the Sky, and outrageous.

But there are positive alternatives, not in some halcyon future, many of which are practiced in Europe and Canada, and even in some companies in the U.S. Our European and Canadian friends bring to us their experience in identifying problems and finding solutions.

We office workers are significant in today's society. We are the largest sector of the workforce, and the fastest growing. In fact, clerical and service work are virtually the only expanding sectors of the workforce. No longer is the typical American worker a man in a hardhat. The typical worker is now a woman at a typewriter—or, rather, a keyboard.

And we have significant problems. Our pay is at the bottom of the payscale. With average pay at around $11,000, we earn less than every kind of blue collar workers. A skilled secretary earns less than a parking lot attendant.

Our lifetimes of work—and women work nearly their whole lives— lead to a retirement of poverty. Ninety percent of women in private industry retire without a penny in pension benefits.

But the statistics only blur the reality. A clerical worker at John Hancock was forced to give up custody of her child when the judge ruled her full-time salary was inadequate to support a family. A Minnesota school secretary with 14 years experience earns less than the boy who puts the groceries in her car.

These are the problems of "women's work"—the low-paid, low-prestige, dead-end jobs that most women hold.

Will this continue? Where do we find the solutions to these problems?

Automation provides opportunities to find solutions to all these problems. But there is a dual nature to automation, like Dr. Jekyll and Mr. Hyde. And the question is, will automation be implemented to bring about a future that is better or worse for office workers?

Office automation can and should be used to enhance jobs; provide opportunities for advancement of women clericals; increase productivity; provide a healthier work environment; and improve our standard of living.

The rhetoric sounds good. The magazines like to write about the paperless office. The TV reports like to show the robots that deliver the mail. The systems analysts like to talk about how the machines will enhance the work of high level personnel. And the advertisers like to depict the happy ending of the frightened secretary overcoming her Freudian fears and learning to love her word processor.

But how does automation look from the bottom of the office hierarchy?

A Los Angeles legal secretary finds that much of the repetitive typing is eliminated from her job, and she's thrilled.

An Atlanta secretary has found many innovative uses for the computer in her office, and was promoted to reflect her increased level of responsibility.

But a New York word processor tells of being unable to focus her eyes to read when she gets home from work, a bitter disappointment because she loves to read.

A keypunch operator in New Hampshire gets a splitting headache every day, and finds herself screaming at her kids all the time.

And a Cleveland data entry clerk tells me "I've been doing this job for 10 years and I've been tired for 10 years. It's the monotony that does it. I'd like to know what it feels like not to be tired."

Office workers know there are problems. And so do many in management. A bank executive chuckled as he described the data bank operations to me, and said, "I don't know how they can stand those jobs."

Yes, though the computer age presents us with technological progress, it confronts society with grave dangers, dangers that all of us should be concerned about. Our task is to chart a way to turn these dangers into opportunities—opportunities for social progress.

The first threat is to the quality of jobs, and the opportunity is to create new jobs that are more interesting, varied, challenging. When new technology is brought in, it is usually accompanied by rationalizing the jobs. Each job is broken down into its smallest possible component, and new jobs are created. The new jobs repeat the same task, over and over.

I know because I worked at a job like that. I worked as a terminal operator at an insurance company. My job consisted of typing one line of letters and numbers from a green form into the terminal; then typing the line of letters and numbers from another green form; and another, and another, and another. That was my job for 7 1/2 hours a day. You don't have to be a college graduate to hate that kind of work.

Though manufacturers say that centralizing tasks and rationalizing jobs is a thing of the past, the evidence remains—when clerical jobs are automated, two low level jobs are created for every higher level job. Millions of women work under these conditions, and millions more will in the future.

We shouldn't be surprised that managers expect something better from their automated jobs, and that manufacturers are trying to accomodate them. As clericals, we need to decide what we want, and demand that our jobs be made better, too.

But because we are creating new jobs, we have an unprecedented opportunity to design them well. The Worker Protection and Working Environment Act in Norway calls for an end to monotonous work; recommends that the professional advancement of the workers be considered in designing jobs; and that workers should have contact with each other, not just with machines; and that jobs be integrated with each other. These are some of the things we'd like to see in our jobs of the future.

Will automation recapitulate and further entrench the pattern of discrimination in employment, or will it bring in a new era of Pay Equity?

Discrimination characterizes the American workforce of today. Women are concentrated in a few low-paying job categories. According to a recent report from the Bureau of Labor Statistics, women earn considerably less than men in every job category. And despite nearly 20 years of legislated equality, minorities earn less than whites across the board.

Sadly, the new automated jobs repeat the same pattern of discrimination. Seventy-five percent of the high-paid, high prestige jobs are men; 75% of the low-paid, low-prestige jobs are women, and the lowest ranks are disproportionately filled by minorities. Discrimination is often explained as a legacy of the past. Now we see the jobs of the future locking that legacy in place permanently.

But automation means a whole new job structure will come into place, with a whole new vista of jobs. This is a unique opportunity to break the pattern of discrimination in employment for good. New jobs could be paid on the basis of their worth, not the gender of the worker. Job ladders can be built that encourage upward mobility, using real job qualifications for promotion, and not outdated degrees. Automation may be one of the few viable strategies for achieving pay equity for women—a strategy that blends justice with future growth.

If loss of limb and back strain are the characteristic occupational hazards of the industrial age, then job stress is the characteristic hazard of the computer age. It's an insidious hazard, because it's hard to identify, and as Americans we frown on what we consider to be a personality weakness. But stress is not in your head, it's in the office. And it could be a blight on our society.

The Framingham Heart Study released in 1980 showed that women clericals with blue collar husbands and children had a heart disease rate that was twice as high as that of men. The reasons? "Economic stress"—I call it no money; unsupportive bosses; lack of decision-making; and dead-end jobs.

What does the automated future hold? The worst vision includes the Video Display Terminal that monitors the worker automatically and sets the pace of work, counts errors, and reports keystrokes—by the week, by the day, by the hour, by the minute. That has to be the ultimate "unsupportive boss" and the death of decision-making.

When jobs are downgraded and rationalized, clericals earn less for more work. And jobs hold even less future for advancement.

A 1981 NIOSH study proved the point. NIOSH found that clericals working full-time on VDT's had the highest rate of stress ever reported—higher even than most air-traffic controllers.

Either we heed the warnings, or we pay the price. And the price will be paid by individuals.

But the office of the future could reduce stress, and provide a healthy working environment. Union agreements in Austria limit continuous work on a VDT to four hours a day. Throughout Europe, rest breaks after every few hours of work on a VDT are required. In Sweden, productivity is measured for a department's output, not an individual worker's, and by the month, not the hour. And in Canada, where there is a concern about the possible emission of harmful X-rays from VDTs, pregnant workers can be transferred away from the machine for the duration of their pregnancy.

Long-term structural unemployment is the next danger—job loss. After all, the purpose of automation is to reduce labor costs. And though we at 9 to 5 don't oppose automation as such on these grounds, as a society we must look at the future we are creating. European studies predict as much as 20% unemployment among clericals in 15 years.

The U.S. doesn't make the same predictions—not because conditions here are so different, but because the Department of Labor doesn't yet have a method for revising employment predictions based on automation.

This isn't a problem only for office workers. We have undergone a change over the last 50 years—a sharp decline in manufacturing jobs being replaced by lower paid clerical and service jobs. But when the clerical jobs go, what will replace them?

New technology agreements throughout Europe require advance notification of workers of disruptive technological changes; job training for displaced workers; and participation by workers in planning.

Finally, we are concerned about productivity. The purpose of automation is to improve productivity, and anyone who has corrected a manuscript on a word processor as opposed to a conventional typewriter can attest to success.

But some elements work against increased productivity, especially who—or what—controls the pace of work. Studies show that error rates can increase 40 - 400% when the work pace is set by the machine. And NIOSH is finding that job satisfaction and performance improve when workers control the pace of work.

Our society is technologically advanced. We put people on the moon; we build nuclear arsenals able to destroy the world many times over; we've got typewriters that listen and telephones that see. Surely we can reach the relatively smaller goals of building safe machines, designing good jobs, providing for career advancement, increasing productivity, and preventing job loss.

Not only can we, we have to. For what is our future if it is the demon Mr. Hyde that symbolizes the office of the future? A workforce characterized by alienation. An army of working poor who become a majority. Massive unemployment. That's not stability. A sane society doesn't plan to go in that direction.

Conclusion

On my trip to Europe this summer, I became discouraged in comparing the progress in the United States on these issues to the progress in Europe. But my hosts pointed out that Americans have a great advantage, in our ingenuity and brashness. And I came to realize that we do have the ability to use our technological progress for social progress.

I hope this conference helps establish a new debate and a new era. The old questions are answered—there are problems associated with automation. The new questions remain before us—how to turn the dangers into opportunities.

It's up to all of us to live up to the promise and not the threat of the office of the future.

Bargaining Over the Social Costs of Information Technology*

Claudio Ciborra
Dipartimento di Elettronica
Politechnico di Milano, Italy

This paper will discuss the issues of user participation, and relate them to the distribution of social costs of information technology.

There is a debate in Europe on the issue of user participation in technological change, especially when information technology is being applied. There are different kinds of experiences: technology agreements, especially in Northern Europe; company negotiations in most European countries, for example in Italy in companies such as FIAT and Olivetti. The arguments raised for and against participation in technological change usually are very much value-loaded, with the character of a "moral issue," whether from the union or the management or the specialists' point of view.

What I will present here is a hard-nosed economic approach to the whole matter. The results of this economic analysis are the following: First, if technological change is inevitable, so is bargaining over technological change. Management can ignore the equity issues raised by unions; unions can ignore the efficiency problems raised by manage-

*The theoretical framework developed here is derived from my paper presented at the International Federation of Information Processors Conference on System Design, Riva del Sol, Italy, September 1982.

ment. But the economic forces around technological change are at work despite reciprocal ignorance of the actors concerned.

Second, different alternatives to participation in bargaining over technological change can be evaluated on the basis of efficiency of the bargaining process.

Generating Social Costs

Let me start the analysis on the following assumption: that information technology creates social costs. That is, an economic agent consuming new technology for its productive purposes may affect other agents, who are in direct or indirect contact with the technology. (One person's consumption may enter into other people's utility.)

There is the consumption by management, of companies, of information technology for increasing the productivity of publicity work, for example, in the case of office automation. The consumption of this new technology creates side effects, which can be positive and beneficial, and which can be also negative for various user groups.

It is something like pollution, a well-known case of an externality provoked by industrial processes. An innovation in a chemical plant, for example, can increase the productivity of the plant in terms of its production processes. But it also carries side effects, both for the company and outside. So you have all the problems of how to allocate the "social costs" of the pollution created by the plant.

I would argue that information technology is a similar case. Information technology, besides increasing productivity, can "pollute" the organization in various ways. Many of the negative consequences originated by the introduction of computer systems can be regarded as externalities. Inside the organization, computers effect decision-making, control and autonomy, the qualifications of blue- and white-collar workers, the pace of work, and the health and safety of those working on the terminals. All these effects can be classified as externalities or social costs that lead to pollution of the information technology within the organization, and also to clients and customers outside the organization.

Some of these effects are unavoidable consequences of the increase in productivity brought by computers. But more often the effects are the outcome of design choices, and thus are not determined unequivocally by the hardware.

The employment relation is governed by a contract according to which the employee accepts the giving up of the right to govern his or her productive behavior during the working day, and accepts for that period the authority of the employer to sequentially specify the actions he or she must perform—to control those actions so that they are executed according to the employer's plans, in exchange for a set of tangible and intangible rewards.

Computer-based information systems, irregardless of the precise tasks to which they are dedicated, allow the employer to perform more sharply the planning, monitoring and controlling of work, thus altering the implicit or explicit balance embedded in the execution of the traditional employment contract. The preexisting level of perceived equity may thus be disturbed or break down as a direct result of the new computer-based system. This may lead to the well-known phenomenology of resistance to the systems, underutilization of them, and the lack of acceptance among employees at the various levels of the organization.

Internalization Through Bargaining

Once you assume that the implementation of computer technology does indeed generate social costs, there is naturally a problem that has to be dealt with: how to allocate to society the costs and benefits produced by the new technology, that is the benefits of the new productivity and the costs in the changes in work organization and quality.

Historically, what happens is a process of internalization of the social costs. Internalizing social costs scattered among various individuals means converting a cost which is difficult to fix and allocate into something measurable and allocable at a sufficiently low bargaining cost. Somehow these costs and benefits have to be allocated and taken into account. If you ignore them, what you have is an economic system which is not so productive as it could be, and where equality is not as high as it could be.

How does the internalization of social costs take place? Basically it takes place through bargaining processes among the parties affected: management, unions, users, and citizens. Of course negotiations and bargaining can be a very complex task, especially if these social costs are difficult to assess, to identify, to talk about, to allocate. So what do we need? For the sake of a more equitable and more productive work system we need a more just and efficient development process around new technology.

Let me use an example here. Consider an economic system based on slavery, and compare this with a system based on wage labor. Both systems have existed or do exist. The system based on slave labor is characterized by the following dimensions: very cheap labor, rather low productivity, and very high inequality. The labor is cheap because the owners pay the slaves' cost of living and nothing else. High inequality is obvious; there are different groups in the society, one that can dispose of personal freedom and one that cannot. And then, low productivity because of the large amount of social costs of slavery, and these costs are not explicit.

Now let's suppose one changes the legal rights' system by abolishing slavery. This may happen in the following way. At a certain moment slaves can buy their own freedom by giving a certain amount of money to their owners. Following that, slaves sell their labor in exchange for wages. Then a system exists that has higher productivity, not as high inequality, and higher labor costs. The higher labor costs here are due to the fact , that in the new system the social costs have been made explicit, and have been allocated to various groups across the society. Thus the internalization of social costs takes place through some kind of bargaining process in the wage-labor market.

Given a particular set of social costs, the problem of internalization is to find the best institutional arrangement of property rights that allows the allocation of social costs so that the total product yield by that arrangement is maximized. I put forward that this approach also applies in the case of information technology and the bargaining issue over the design of systems, and that "user participation" can be justified within this type of process.

Forms of Participation in System Design

It is now possible to reconsider the issue of participation on new foundations. The interests of individuals and groups bearing externalities will be taken into account only to the extent that the organization is exposed to the demands of those individuals, and to the degree that some influence can overcome the incentives of organizations to resist and buffer demands for change. As explained above, internalizing social costs due to the use of information technology requires bargaining among the parties affected. In this context, three situations can be illustrated.

The first alternative is to ignore bargaining and to insist that information technology has no social costs. In this case the right to use information resides exclusively in the hands of management, who dispose of its consequences by fiat. The employees are required to adapt and to follow instruction from the top regarding changes in their work organization.

This "no formal bargaining" alternative was thought to be the most efficient solution for introducing computers before the user participation theme was developed. At the extreme, proponents of this view claimed that computers had no impact on the work organization, qualifications, employment, etc. But inefficiencies emerged in the various forms we are familiar with: user resistance; adaptation problems; local and/or global conflicts during and after computerization; slow down in project execution: and so on. Frequently such problems were attributed to the user's psychology, and thus are considered to be outside the domain of rational organizational behavior that could be controlled by management.

In the perspective outlined here, these forms of resistance reflect inefficiencies related to the very rational process of internalization of social costs. (Recall the slavery example where cheap labor went along with low productivity.) As mentioned above, informatics affects the balance embedded in employment relations. If equity does not obtain anymore, then employees will withhold effort in various ways, mainly by exploiting the uncertainties of the new technology. They can, for example, refuse to tap their knowledge and skills to the formal procedures running on the new system, thus hindering its efficacy. The opportunistic use of job knowledge is the rational reaction to the perception of inequity in the employment contract brought by the increased sharpness in monitoring and control.

Resistance can arise at any point in the organization: individuals, groups, or organizational units can block the whole system, or more frequently can lower its efficacy. As a consequence, individual bargains regulated by ad hoc contracts must be struck continuously by the organization with different parties in order to continue the development of the system. As a result of this, latent bargaining costs rise.

The second alternative is to make the social costs of information technology explicit through contracts and agreements. This is the case in the Scandinavian countries, where the development of systems is bargained explicitly between the unions and management. In the present perspective, the object of such contracts is to achieve a rearrangement in the property rights related to systems and data. More specifically, the property rights concern (a) the system development process, and (b) the use of the system once implemented. A first and very important consequence of the agreements or "contracts" is to "unfreeze" the existing management rights or prerogatives concerning who has the property of technological change.

This type of bargaining of course makes the design effort longer and more costly. But think back to the slave example. The costs of negotiated design must appear in order to make explicit some of the social costs related to the implementation of information technology. So, often the design process is longer and more troublesome because one negotiates each specific system. But in the end systems are productive, accepted and used by the users.

Government Regulation

The third alternative is state regulation through legislation. The state intervenes and affects the system in terms of the design process. Given the high bargaining costs related to technological change, regulation does have an impact on the application of computers and the organization of computer-based tasks. Establishing regulations thus should be done considering the economic impact of the resulting legal arrangement. Making either the employer or the employees totally liable for the externalities could not be the optimal solution, at least from a global point of view.

Because it provides organizations with the incentives to reduce the social costs borne by individuals inside and outside the organization, regulation represents a means to force them to alter their structures, rules and norms so as to better internalize those costs.

Regulation is the means to modify the status quo, the inertia due to the impossibility for large groups to influence organizations. But there are difficulties in using regulation for that purpose. For one thing, regulation is emanated by a political body, and the representation of interests within this body can be problematic. In addition, the difficulties in organizing a collective action may be shifted from the economic arena to the political one. For another, regulation may be too general, and, in many cases, generic because of its comprehensiveness. In fact, either very specific aspects are regulated because of the existence of standards (e.g. working time at VDUs), or simply "principles" are stated. Also, regulation is rigid. And the time needed to prepare, implement and evaluate rules is longer than the pace of technological change. Regulation implicitly based on the problems related to a large, centralized EDP center may be totally irrelevant for a decentralized office automation system. Finally, costs of enforcement have to be faced.

Conclusion

My appraisal has not stated ultimately what arrangement is the most efficient and effective at internalizing social costs. This determination probably depends on the contingencies related to the development of a specific system. What is certain is the inefficiency of disregarding a comparative analysis, in the context of a specific situation, of the alternatives available.

Consequently, let me spend my concluding remarks in favor of the last two alternatives, that is, explicitly bargaining around technological change and in some cases state legislation. Why do I favor, from the efficiently and equity points of views, these two alternatives? Because both of these alternative unfreeze the existing legal system, the status quo of unilateral management prerogatives regarding systems design and the property rights over computer systems. These alternatives are the only ones that allow a free bargaining of technological change. In the end, the system being designed will reflect the power and strength of the parties involved in the negotiations and not simply an obsolete state of affairs.

The point of my analysis is that there should be a framework where negotiations are allowed, both for the sake of efficiency and for the sake of equity.

Literature

Brooks, H. **Science, Technology and Society in the 1980s,** in Science and Technology Policy for the 80s, OECD, Paris, 1981.

Ciborra, C. **The Social Costs of Information Technology and Participation in Systems Design,** in U. Briefs, C. Ciborra, L. Schneider (Editors), Systems Design By the Users, With the Users, For the Users, North-Holland Pub. Co., Amsterdam, 1983.

Reese, J. et al., **Technische Rationalisierung und Extermalisierung von Kosten in Oeffentlichen Bereich,** Gesamthochschule Kassel, 1981.

Salomon, J.J., **Promethee empetre,** Pergamon Press, Paris, 1981.

II. Employment Impacts
of
Office Computerization

Women, Technological Change and Employment Levels:
The Role of Trade Union Policies

Helga Cammell
International Federation of Commercial,
Clerical, Professional and Technical Employees
FIET, Switzerland

On behalf of my international organization, FIET, and its over 7 1/2 million members all over the world, 45% of which are women, in 80 countries, from 180 unions; and on behalf of FIET's General Secretary, Heribert Maier, I greet you. Despite a very heavy work load within my own international, I have accepted the invitation to speak here because I believe that this conference, at this stage, is a necessity, and I whole-heartedly congratulate the organizers.

The introduction of the new microelectronic technology in the service sectors has far-reaching effects on the nature and organization of work, and thereby on the employment, on the professional qualifications, and on the health of workers.

Especially affected are industry, commerce, insurance and banking, the sectors where FIET members are employed. Particular occupations involving average qualifications and simple activities such as word processing and data collection and clerical duties, are increasingly being subject to rationalization. The resulting danger: the abolition of posts and the downgrading of qualifications.

With respect to the actual general unemployment situation in the OECD, we have figures for the European OECD countries. In the first half of 1982, there were more than 16 million people registered as unemployed—almost 10% of the working population. And in the developing countries, as you may know, the situation is far worse.

The economic damage which this is doing, both in terms of lost output and depressed living standards, is evident; not to mention the social damage.

As far as women are concerned, the group which participates over-proportionately among the unemployed, who constitute an average of 1/3 of the labor force, they accounted for 45% of the unemployed in the third quarter of 1981, in the EEC and OECD. Women even outnumbered unemployed men in eight European countries.

Job Creation or Displacement?

The effects of technological change on employment are difficult to measure. There are many factors to take into account. It is however, believed that new technology will accelerate job loss and that the job loss effects of new technology will outweigh the job creation effect if appropriate measures are not taken.

During a recent international survey, many unions reported that the labor-intensive office is a prime target for investment in rationalization measures. We have an example from the large American multinational bank, CitiBank, which has stated that their management has had to recognize that the back office was really a factory, and not a clerical function. For them, the issue has been to reverse the ratio of labor costs, previously 70%, to hardware and software costs.

According to a very wide-reported and quoted report by Siemens, which covered 2.7 million office jobs, it was found that 43% of the jobs could be standardized, and 25% to 30% automated. The EC, the European Commission, in 1980 estimated that up to 1990, approximately 20-25% of the then current 15 million office jobs in the European Community—that means 3 to 3.75 million jobs—are expected to be affected by the elimination of certain unqualified functions.

Concerning future trends in employment, FIET, my organization, states that if productivity increases significantly due to the introduction of new technology, then there must be an even greater expansion in output to compensate. Otherwise, total employment will fall.

Concerning the prospects for growth in output over the next few years, FIET emphasizes that the deflationary, monetaristic economic policies currently being implemented by certain leading economies, including the United States, cause disastrous fall in output rather than growth. And as an unpublished report by the International Confederation of Free Trade Unions and International Trade Secretariats (ICFTU/ITS) mentions, the commission of the EEC has estimated that return to full employment will require an annual growth rate in the EEC countries of at least 5% per annum over the next 5 years. The growth rate for 1981 in OECD countries was only 1.25%, and is projected to continue at about that rate.

According to the European Trade Union Institute (ETUI), almost 15 million new jobs would have to be created in the EEC countries from 1980 to 1985, to lower the unemployent rate to 2% from 5.5% rate in mid-1979. Today it is around 11%.

According to forecasts, the job creation effects of new technology are unlikely to outweigh the job displacement effects. The ETUI has estimated that the impact of microelectronics on output will lead to relatively few jobs being created. The American management consultant organization, Arthur D. Little, has estimated that in the next ten years in four countries (U.S.A., UK, France and Germany), only one million jobs will be created, 60% of which will be located in the United States.

Women's Position in the Computer Job Hierarchy

What computer-related office jobs are likely to be created? Here it is very difficult to state actual numbers. The ICFTU/ITS report mentions the Cambridge University study which estimates that by by 1983, 40,000 additional jobs could be created in the administrative, managerial, professional and technical group in the United Kingdom. On the other hand, the U.S. Department of Labor has estimated that clerical work will be the fastest growing occupation in the '80s, with almost 5 million new jobs, and presumably this includes word processor operators.

Although there will be a certain amount of job creation, these jobs will not absorb women at the same rate as men. The segregation of women into less skilled jobs at the bottom of the hierarchy is likely to continue. Women are less likely than men to take up technical training and therefore will find it difficult to move into the higher-level and better paid jobs.

Computer programming occupations were defined right from the start as technical and professional, and therefore became predominantely male. Women, it seems, will be confined to word processor operation, and possibly supervision.

Another trend that has been commented upon is the predominance of women in certain job categories. This has been due to the deskilling and downgrading of jobs, as well as the substitution of electronic equipment in place of personal judgement. These trends just entrench women in lower-level jobs.

Other trends, such as more part-time and shift work, also discriminate against women, making it difficult for them to receive further training and promotion. Several FIET affiliates also express deep concern about the introduction of work at home in the FIET sectors. The introduction of VDU screen terminals in the "home" would, for example, represent a new challenge to the trade union movement with respect to the trade union organization of the workers concerned—probably mostly women—and their social protection. In connection with decentralization of work, the Commission of the European Communities also expects an "extension of home work."

Structural Unemployment and New Technology

FIET concludes that the biggest economic and social problem facing the world today is unemployment. The immediate cause of the current shocking level of unemployment is the recessionary economic policies being pursued by the governments in most European countries, the United States, and other industrialized nations. High interest rates, cutbacks in the capital spending of governments, and attacks on Social Security programs have contributed to falls in industrial production and national income.

The current recession, however, as serious as it is, is not the only reason for the current high unemployment. Over the past 10 years or more there has been a growth in the underlying rate of unemployment caused by structural changes. The factors causing these changes must be eliminated if full employment is to be achieved.

FIET stresses that one of the most important structural developments affecting Europe is the uncontrolled, rapid acceleration of the use of new technologies, both in the manufacturing and service sectors.

In this connection, we have to mention multinational companies. They use their own easy access to the very latest available information technology, and so increase their power vis a vis governments and employees.

For the union movement, therefore, there is a program which must be pursued at the level of individual companies, with employers' associations, with local authorities, national governments, and with international organizations.

Trade Union Policies

The chief features of trade union policy on technological change and employment, some of which have been written in new technology agreements, are as follows:

●**Governments must ensure that the introduction of new technology** is not left to the market forces. Governments must control the rate of the introduction of new technology and monitor its impact on employment and working conditions.

At the same time, governments must pursue full employment. Any redundancies should be compensated for by creating new jobs in other sectors, especially in the public sector.

Also, governments should create a favorable climate for employment changes. Redeployed staff should suffer no loss of grade or income, and should receive adequate allowances for relocation.

Further, governments must ensure the extension of industrial democracy, consultation, negotiation, and information rights of trade unions with respect to technology.

Concerning information disclosure, management must disclose all information relevant to decision making, planning, and implementation of technological change to trade union representatives prior to any decision making.

● **All technological changes must be negotiated with the union and cannot be implemented without union agreement.** All of the unions must also arrive at agreements with employers and competent public bodies on retraining programs for workers -women as well as men — whose jobs are threatened by new technology or who need an additional training for the purposes of obtaining access to the new occupations which new technology has brought into existance.

My international is in the process of setting up an international model technology agreement to be used by FIET affiliates. This will emphasize that trade unions have to give employment creation top priority in their collective bargaining strategies, and while defending achieving standards, must examine their other policies, so that they insure that these policies are consistent with employment creation.

● **Reliance on the protection of existing jobs is not sufficient.** In view of the massive technological and structural changes taking place today, reductions in working time can be an important method of reconciling the likely growth in output and productivity, so as to produce rising employment. At the same time, reduced working time can provide a massive step forward in improving the working conditions of salaried employees.

Governments must accept that working time reduction can be an important weapon—though not the only one—in the fight against unemployment, and should take steps to encourage reductions in working time, both as a social and an economic measure.

The most vulnerable group, women, need special attention. It is working women who have understood the serious situation that has arisen also due to the introduction of new office technology, and are affiliating in a greater number than ever before in their respective FIET unions in countries all over the world.

Government Policies on New Information Technologies and Their Implications for Employment: An Overview of EEC Countries, With Particular Reference to Women

Christine Zmroczek & Felicity Henwood
Science Policy Research Unit
University of Sussex, Great Britain

As a result of research we conducted for the European Commission, we gained an overall impression of the government initiatives that were being taken in European Economic Community (EEC) countries on new technology and employment. We will present here an overview of the governmental responses to the introduction of new technologies in Europe, bearing in mind the effects that these responses will have for employment and in particular for women's employment.

We begin by discussing the initiatives taken by the European Commission in this context and then go on to outline some actions taken by the individual member states vis-a-vis new technologies.

A Commitment to Equal Opportunities

At the European level, the European Community has a longstanding commitment to improve the situation of women in the EEC, particularly in employment matters. In 1974, the Social Action Programme expressed the political will to achieve equality between women and men as regards access to employment, training and conditions of employment. This programme gave rise to three Council Directives concerning the approximation of the laws of the member states relating to the application of the principle of equal pay for women and men (1975); the implementation of the principle of equal treatment for women and men as regards access to employment, vocational training and promotion, and working conditions (1976); and concerning the progressive implementation of the principle of equal treatment for women and men in matters of social security (1978).

These legal instruments have played an important role in stimulating action by the member states and have hastened the adoption of national legislation in this field, such as acts concerning sexual discrimination and equal pay.

The Community's financial instruments—in particular the European Social Fund—are aimed at contributing to the achievement in practice of equal opportunities for women and men. A Council decision of December 1977 concerned intervention by the E.S.F. to provide "financial support for special training measures designed to afford access by women to jobs where they (sic) have traditionally been under represented". (Commission of European Communities, 1981, p.2). The European Social Fund's aim is the desegregation of employment, this being recognized as an important first step towards the achievement of equal opportunities in the member states.

The Community is aware of the need for sustained action over a long period if equal opportunities for women and men are to be attained. The Community sees itself as taking a central role in improving the situation of women, not only through legal measures providing for equal treatment, especially in employment, but also by complementing these measures with diverse forms of "positive action". There is also growing concern that policies should be continually adapted to take account of the changing economic and social circumstances prevailing in the 1980's as compared with the previous decade.

As a result of these concerns, the Commission has published the **Community Action Programme on the Promotions of Equal Opportunities for Women, 1982-1985** (Commission of the European Communities, 1981). In this document, Action 10 is concerned with the integration of women into working life, in particular, with respect to the new technologies. The aim of Action 10 is "to promote the diversification of occupational choices for women and the mastering of new technologies with particular reference to guidance and initial and continual training". (Commission of the European Communities, 1981)

Special Training Initiatives

The Communities' Programme recognizes that setting up training programmes for women is not, of itself, enough, and discusses the need to break down the traditional stereotyped view of woman's role, including the belief that technical occupations are not 'feminine'. Member states are encouraged to undertake, continue or reinforce positive measures to improve equal opportunities in education, guidance and training, including: encouraging women to enter non-traditional occupations; improving women's access to jobs other than unskilled jobs (especially those involving use of new technologies); training vocational guidance counsellors to make them aware of need for diversification in career choices for girls and boys (paying particular attention to needs of immigrant girls); and training women with a view to re-integration into working life after a break.

The Commission's action is being extended through the European Social Fund and in liaison with the European Centre for the Development of Vocational Training (CEDEFOP). Some examples of projects funded by the ESF and aimed at promotion of equal opportunities by encouraging women to train for the more technical jobs are: in Italy—programmes to train women in computer analysis and programming occupations; in France—programmes for women in office automation; and in the U.K., the East Leeds Women's Workshop, funded jointly by ESF and Leeds City Council, which instructs women in electronics and computing skills. This project is aimed at women over the age of 25 years, who may have children and have been unemployed for some time.

Another recent communication from the Commission deals with new information technology and vocational training and the new Community initiatives for 1983-1987. It recommends measures to supplement and strengthen vocational training in the member states and stresses the need for a socially sensitive and responsible policy for the introduction of information technologies which is at the same time, fully responsive to economic and technical needs.

The Commission's proposals, which will be put before the Council in the next few months, prioritize four main areas:

   (i) The training needs of small and medium size enterprises seeking to apply new technology and planning them on the basis of consensus with all employees.

  (ii) The implications of in-house training in large scale enterprises in the service sector which seek to introduce automated administration and management techniques (for instance in banking and retailing), with consideration of positive action towards those whose skills become redundant.

 (iii) The scope of new information technology as a learning tool for unqualified unemployed young people.

 (iv) How to adapt and update the skills of those made redundant in manufacturing industry, particularly in steel.

A network of pilot projects will be set up in these areas to run over the next 4 years, with a coordinated structure for the exchange of ideas and experience between countries. In this way it is intended to lay the foundation for more practical measures in the medium term.

Emphasis is also laid on general public awareness about new information technologies and the need for efforts to familiarize people with its potential through non-vocational adult and continuing education and the mass-media. In compulsory education, the Communication emphasizes a major commitment of the Commission as a whole to the encouragement of special efforts to integrate and improve the awareness of new information technologies in traditional education. Particular attention is to be paid to teacher training, educationally sound computer programmes, firsthand experience in working with computers, and improvement in the transition from education to working life.

Government Policies in the Member Countries

We will now briefly outline government actions regarding new technologies in member states and their implications for employment, particularly women's employment. We discuss government sponsored research and government education and training initiatives as well as the more explicit government statements regarding policies for new technologies which seem relevant. Much of our information is based on a survey of the European Commission's series, **Social Change and Technology in Europe,** by the European Pool of Studies (EPOS), in itself a very useful publication, regularly bringing together contributions from the European Community countries regarding government, employer and union actions in relation to the development of information technologies.

We are giving an overview of the European situation and acknowledge that some of the information may now be out of date; published material lags behind initiatives actually being taken, and recent changes in government have meant significant policy changes in some cases. For instance, in Germany, the government has changed in the last few weeks and we have yet to receive any detailed information on how this will affect policies on new technology.

The late 70's saw the publication of several major government-sponsored projects concerning micro-electronics technology.

These included: the Nora-Minc Report in France; the Siemens Report in Germany; the Rathenau Report in the Netherlands; the National Council for the Promotion of Sciences Report in Belgium; the National Board for Science and Technology Report in Ireland; and the ACARD Report in the U.K. These reports provided general overviews of the situation vis-a-vis microelectronics technology in each country, and some made recommendations to their (respective) governments.

Other government initiatives were also taken around this time. For instance, in the U.K. the Microelectronics Awareness Programme (MAP) allocated L25m to increase industrial awareness and training, to provide consultancy support to companies and to help develop applications of electronics. The Microelectronics Industry Support Programme (MISP) had L55m to support the manufacture of microelectronic components and devices. Similar promotion activities were taking place in other countries at the same time.

The promotion activities pursued by governments around this time reflected their conviction about the inevitability of microelectronics technology in the highly competitive world of advanced capitalism. Governments and individual firms were aware that not introducing the technologies was likely to mean falling behind their competitors which would, as was often pointed out to the trade unions, ultimately result in job loss. Governments therefore accepted that new technologies should be promoted.

At this point, employment and unemployment issues become a focus of attention. While governments remain loathe to admit that large scale unemployment might be more than a short-term consequence of the introduction of new technologies, they nevertheless are aware that there are important social and economic implications that have to be taken into consideration in future policies.

The period 1979-1980 saw several large-scale government sponsored studies examining the social implications of micro-electronics. In the UK, Boatwright, Sleigh, et al. prepared a report for the Department of Employment which optimistically concluded that the effects of the microelectronics would be no more severe, in terms of job loss, than previous examples of technological change. The Rathenau Report on the social consequences of microelectronics in the Netherlands, was slightly more cautious in its approach. In advising the Dutch government, the report recommended that the government should have an active, regulatory role vis-a-vis new technologies and in particular should devise special policies regarding education, work and employment.

One of the results of these general studies on the social implications of microelectronics has been the sponsorship by governments of projects and research that focus on some of the more specific implications highlighted by them, at the same time as efforts to promote the new technologies continue.

In Germany, for example, the government set aside about DM650m for projects on the Humanization of the Working Environment Programme between 1974 and 1981. The money has been used to fund projects concerned mostly with health and safety at work. The overall aim of the programme has been to ensure that advanced technologies can be used without there being any deterioration in the conditions of work. (In some cases this has resulted in projects that involved participation by employees in decisions concerning the implementation of new technology; we have heard of at least one example of that.) Several reports and papers have already been published as a result of this initiative.

While such action on the part of governments must be applauded and encouraged, it is often hard to see if the results of these relatively specific research projects are actually affecting government policies overall. Statements from the former government in Germany, especially those from the Minister of Research and Technology, von Bulow, still tended to concentrate on the promotion of information technology and its job creation aspects at the expense of discussing some of the less positive social implications.

Continued Promotional Activities

Similar examples can be found in other EEC countries. In France, the socialist government that came to power in 1981 has made great efforts to ensure that the wider social and economic consequences of introducing microelectronics are assessed and taken seriously. In particular, the Department of Information (Mission a la Informatique) in collaboration with the National Agency for the Amelioration of Working Conditions (A.N.A.C.T.) has produced a guide to the issues of quality of work resulting from the introduction of new technologies. In the promotion of information technology, however, the French government has been very keen to stress the positive aspects. In announcing the setting up of the World Centre for the Social Uses of Microprocessors in Paris in November 1981, President Mitterand stated:

" . . .information technology could play a significant role in the evolution of our society . . . if we adopt an intelligent approach to the introduction of information technology in the context of an overall plan for society, it could expand every individual's capacity to work and to create." So, whilst the government is aware of some of the more negative social implications of the technology, the overall policy seems to be one of 'go ahead', with the 'World Centre' being used to promote the idea that microelectronic technology is essential for industrial and technological renovation.

In the U.K., a similar promotion exercise has been undertaken by the Conservative government in 1982 — appropriately named 'Information Technology Year'. Over Ll million of Government resources were allocated to increase the awareness of the public and of industry to the potentials of new technology and to overcoming suspicions of information technology. The public campaign has attempted to convey the excitement of information technology in the home, at work and elsewhere: schools, banks, shops, libraries, hospitals. The tone has been one of "reassurance" and relatively few questions regarding employment and unemployment have been raised in this campaign.

The industrial campaign, seen as more important by the government, has been positively encouraging firms in the belief that information technology is the key to survival and to the revival of the economy. As David Fairburn, director of the National Computing Centre, put it, "For industry, IT '82 is almost a once-and-for-all opportunity to get its act together," thus conveying the sense of urgency that has been part and parcel of the government's whole campaign.

By drawing together these examples of the promotion exercises being undertaken regarding new information technologies, we are presenting our overall impressions. There is no doubt in our minds that certain elements in the various governments are indeed concerned with the wider social implications associated with the technology, but we believe that, in terms of resource allocation, publicity and action, the emphasis is on the promotion of the new technologies, rather than the assessment of their social implications.

Areas where most governments have been more aware of the need for policies on information technology include education and training. Special programmes have been set up in most EEC countries which aim to train people in the new skills that are needed to work in the information technology age. The problems with most of these programmes is their failure to recognize the needs of specific groups of workers.

Training and Retraining of Women

This failure is highlighted when we come to look at how far training programmes are providing for the special needs of women. We consider this to be fundamentally important at this time when areas of work (particularly office work), where women have traditionally been employed, are now being automated and opportunities for work of a similar skill category are no longer available to women. While governments are aware of the existing inequalities between women and men and have introduced legislation in the area of employment to try to redress some of these imbalances in line with EEC directives (sex discrimination acts, equal pay acts, etc.), these problems are often overlooked when it comes to making specific policies regarding new technologies. The needs of women for training and retraining for example are frequently conflated with those of men. In fact they are often quite different, since women face problems which do not arise merely as a result of new technology but stem from deeply entrenched social values in society.

Although governments are reluctant to acknowledge the extent of these problems and make the changes necessary to overcome many of them, there have been several initiatives taken in recent years aimed at examining, if not alleviating, the problems women face.

In Belgium, in October 1981, the Ministry of Employment and Labour's Female Labour Commission organized a conference on the impact of new technologies upon the employment of women. It was concluded from this conference that the job loss resulting from the introduction of new technologies should not be solved by the introduction of part-time work but through a general reduction in working hours for all workers; that informatics should be on the programme of all technical schools and that additional training of teachers would be needed; that new technologies may lead to more homeworking but that this should not be seen as inevitable because human contact was an important aspect of work, especially for women and that its importance should not be overlooked.

In the Netherlands, the Ministry of Social Affairs and Employment has sponsored a major research project on the social implications of microelectronics on women, now being undertaken at the University of Leiden.

In France, the "Mission a l'Informatique" commissioned a study devoted to the employment of women which is being conducted in collaboration with the Ministry for Women's Rights by The Centre for Research in Industrial Economics (CREI).

In the U.K. a group at the Science Policy Research Unit prepared a report for the Department of Employment on microelectronics and women's employment in Britain. This report is a review of the literature and a discussion of the effects of microelectronics on women's jobs.

A similar exercise, but on a European-wide basis was commissioned by the European Commission in connection with their FAST programme, and was undertaken at SPRU by the authors of this paper. In this report, we surveyed the available literature on the quantitative and qualitative implications of new technologies, and information technologies in particular, for women's employment. We selected and commented on the most significant implications highlighted by the reviewed research projects and defined the existing gaps. Finally, we outlined some of the most important European aspects of problems which would qualify for research at Community level. These recommendations have been included in the recently published report of The Fast Programme (Brussels, September, 1982).

In the course of our research for the EEC report, we were able to amass information about some 400 research projects concerned with new technology and in some way relevant to women's employment. Although only a few of these were the direct result of government initiatives, the increasing interest of the research community in the area of women and new technology reflects the growing awareness of the problems and the commitment on the part of some to devise means of overcoming them.

References

The Advisory Council on Applied Research and Development (A.C.A.R.D.), **The Application of Semi-Conductor Technology,** London 1978.

Clive Cookson, Guide to Information Technology, **The Times,** January 14, 1982.

Commission of the European Communities, **A New Community Action Programme on the Promotion of Equal Opportunities for Women 1982-1985.** Brussels, 1981.

Commission of the European Communities, **Vocational Training and New Information Technologies: New Community Initiatives During the Period 1983-1987.** Brussels, 1982.

European Pool of Studies, **Social Change and Technology in Europe.** Information Bulletins 1-8, Brussels.

Mission a la Informatique, and Agence Nationale pour l'Amelioration des Conditions de Travail (A.N.A.C.T.), **Guide actif Methodologique.** Paris.

National Board for Science and Technology, **Microelectronics: The Implications for Ireland.** NBST, July 1981.

S. Nora and A. Minc, **L'informatisation de la societe.** Documentation Francaise, Paris, 1978.

Prof. G.W. Rathenau, **The Social Consequences of Microelectronics,** Ministerie van Wetenschapsbelend, 1979.

Siemens, Internal Report on the **Impact of Office Technology,** Federal Republic of Germany, 1978.

J. Sleigh, B. Boatwright, P. Irwin and E. Stanyon, **The Manpower Implications of Micro-Electronic Technology,** HMSO, London 1979.

S.P.R.U., Women and Technology Studies, **Microelectronics and Women's Employment in Britain,** SPRU Occasional Paper Series No. 17. SPRU, 1982.

C. Zmroczek-Shannon and F. Henwood, **New Information Technology and Women's Employment.** Final Report EEC (forthcoming).

Training: The Magic Cure
for All Ills?

Robyn Dasey
Banking Insurance & Finance Union, Great Britain

My purpose here is to dispel a number of illusions about the employment situation in the finance industry and about training as a solution to the problem of unemployment resulting both from the current recession, and the implementation of technological change, which is part of company strategy in these circumstances. I argue that training is no answer unless harsh political and economic problems and decisions are faced honestly.

In particular I'm going to address the real problem that we face: what are we training the people for? In other words, are we encouraging people to be trained for jobs that do not exist and will not exist? And what is the purpose of training if there are far too few jobs to fill? What type of skills will be needed if an even higher proportion of the office workforce are in low-skill jobs? The union I speak for here today, the Banking, Insurance & Finance Union (BIFU) in Great Britain, represents 150,000 staff in an industry that is frequently cited as a source of employment growth. It's one of those that all the government reports say is an expanding area of employment, and thus where many of the women and men displaced by technological change from other industries will be able to find work. It is also one of those sectors where the employers argue that the employee will be freed by new technology to do more creative work and provide more extensive customer services.

Employment in UK Banking

First I would like to go into the background of the finance industry in the UK. Employment in UK banks, after rapid growth during the 1960s and early 1970s, tailed off to approximately 2-3% in 1980-81. In Britain, employment levels in the major clearing banks, after rising for many years and then stabilizing, is now declining absolutely. The British banking industry is highly centralized. In 1981-82, the Midland Bank, one of the big four in Britain, declared that it intended to make 2,000 staff "redundant." (Being made redundant means you've been sacked.) For the previous 2 years, along with all of its major competitors, this bank had frozen recruitment except for certain DP posts.

The same trend is apparent in insurance. Only three weeks ago Prudential Assurance announced it was cutting 400 staff in its general household and motor insurance division. The shock of "the Pru" announcing layoffs was so great that the **Financial Guardian** ran an editorial headlined: "Put in a Dedicated Word Processor and You Can Get Rid of Dedicated Staff" (**Guardian,** London, 7 October 1982). Prudential had never before declared a person redundant. Several weeks earlier Commercial Union, another major insurance company, announced the "phasing out" of 1,200 jobs and the "relocating" of many others in satellite offices.

In short, the finance industry, the place where women office workers "phased out" of private manufacturing, distribution and state employment, are told they can get jobs, is itself declining in employment.

Industry Rationalization

Many people ask: "But is this trend due to technology?" The question itself is based on false premises. The application of technology is part and parcel of the employers' strategy. While the major English Clearing Banks admit a reduction of 2,000 staff out of a total of almost 1/4 million in 1981, they state that this is due to general economic and business reasons, not new technology. In saying this they are not being dishonest, but also not totally frank. For technology is implemented as one important component of the "rationalization" of business. They

MAJOR BUSINESS FUNCTIONS AND PROFITABILITY-UK BANKS	
Major Functions	**Profitability** (+ profitable) (− loss)
Domestic Money Transmission	Deposits, potentially + + Transfers − to equal Withdrawals −
Lending: Personal UK Industrial	+ + - to + +
Securities	+ but marginal
International Personal and Corporate Money Transmissions	- to + +
Foreign exch. dealings	+ + +
Foreign Lending: -Business -Governments	- to + + + + + rapidly turning to - Poland, Argentina, Mexico, etc.)

want not only to cut down the labor intensity, but also to reorganize the basic workings of the industry. Thus reorganization and automation are parts of the same package. The jobs mentioned above are being eliminated not solely because of office automation, but because of a total package reorganization of the banking industry.

The chart on the following page illustrates the fundamental business and automation trends of UK banks in aggregate in recent years. You see that money transmission, a fundamental part of the banking industry, is also extremely unprofitable.

Very broadly, the major English banks have been investing most in automating those functions which are fundamental to their business but least profitable and most labor intensive. This has been facilitated by the availability of far lower cost computer systems, but these only inform the basic business decisions, not vice versa.

So what I am arguing is that technology is part of the entire package of how you reorganize an industry. It's part of cutting down labor intensity and it's part of controlling the way those functions are performed.

You may note the parallels between the investment in computerized systems and the summary of the bank's own statement on profitability or otherwise in the previous table. Labor costs comprise about two thirds of total costs in banking in the UK, and the labor cost element is highest in domestic (i.e. the local customer) branch money transactions. Now wouldn't it be so much better, the finance industry says, if we didn't have to provide a person behind a counter who actually would hand out money or take in money and serve the customer? These are precisely the functions that are being automated most rapidly.

The most effective way of providing a customer service with low cost on money transmission is the automatic teller machine. Our people are being told over and over again that they will be spending more time with customer services. In fact staff are not being transferred to customers. The thrust of these efforts is to make the customers do the work themselves—they key in, they put in the information, and so on.

LEVELS OF AUTOMATION RELATED TO MAJOR FUNCTIONS

Domestic

Money Transmission	High investment in ATMs, inter-bank clearing, back office VDTs in local branches. POS (point-of-sale), EFT (electronic fund transfer), pilots especially with petrol stations
Lending	As above plus some banks reorganizing networks of branches. Credit scoring. Variable credit in mag. card systems.
International	Computerized processing of transactions, data base systems, international communications direct link and via SWIFT.

Disappearing Career Paths?

So this is the way these trends are affecting staff. Natural wastage is the term that's used for attrition in Britain. In automating money transmission, we are seeing an enormous impact in the general clerical personnel, as well as in counter staff positions (cashiers) and in the whole of data preparation and the supervision of data input areas. These were the so-called growth areas for women in the 1960s with the introduction of mainframe batch processing.

We are now seeing computer systems that will operate for three and four days on the automatic tellers so that they don't need operators in the central computing location working overnight. Anything that involves counting pieces of paper, whether cash or checks, is in trouble.

So what does this have to do with training? On one level it affects the number of heads that are actually being chopped. Secondly, the promotion paths and recruitment methods in banks is being altered quite drastically.

The chart below shows the current position in the National Westminster Bank, and is typical. It employs approximately 63,000 people, 55% of whom are women. National Westminster is one of Britain's Big Four. If you look at grades 1, 2, 3 and 4 at the bottom, you see they are all women. There are a few men, but very few. Basically, a man joins the bank and if he's got any brains and business acumen whatsoever, he is trained up through accountancy into bank branch manager.

You have a very large number of women in the bottom grade, grade 1, which is supposed to be a temporary grade. You also have a lot in the cashier grade. And then, moving up, women more or less disappear. Women form 75% of the bank staff in the clerical bottom four grades.

Now remember what I said about how the money transmission is affecting jobs. It's cutting back the cashier and general clerical jobs. It's also cutting back the branch managers, because a lot of banks are organized in such a way that a sub- branch will not require anyone of that caliber to manage it. It will be run by an administrative clerk—a more fulfilling job, maybe, but only paying at the bottom of the pay scale.

So I would be very worried if I were a bank manager, to be quite frank, because the men's profile is coming closer and closer to the women's. Not only do we have no upward movement for women, but the men's profile is approaching it as well. With the Midland Bank, for example, when they re-organized their sub-branches, they are cutting back their branch managers by 40%.

This basically means that the promotion ladder, the old system in the banks, is disappearing, and there is nothing else to replace it except for technical specialists, that is, people who are brought in at either accountant's level or who are brought in through the DP departments.

This profile of female employment has developed since the 1960s.

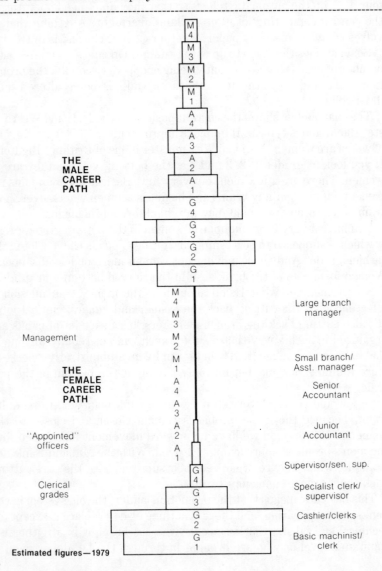

THE MALE CAREER PATH

THE FEMALE CAREER PATH

Management

"Appointed" officers

Clerical grades

Estimated figures—1979

Large branch manager

Small branch/ Asst. manager

Senior Accountant

Junior Accountant

Supervisor/sen. sup.

Specialist clerk/ supervisor

Cashier/clerks

Basic machinist/ clerk

In effect, office technology in banking is being applied in order to, first, reduce the absolute numbers of staff, particularly in money transmission. This will dramatically cut the number of women's cashier and clerical jobs. Secondly, the finance industry wants to reduce the need for human discretion on credit, lending, etc., and concentrate higher-level discretion in fewer and fewer hands. This will dramatically reduce career prospects for men, especially those aspiring to bank branch manager positions.

Women in Banking

UK banks began recruiting women in large numbers in the 1960s. This was part of the major restructuring that led to today's concentration of the Big Four and an extensive and expensive network of branches throughout the country. Women were and are recruited to fill basic cashier and clerical jobs in these local branches.

Now what we are talking about is a wholesale shedding of a large number of women, a very drastic narrowing of the profile. The overall picture is one of a reduced workforce with an even greater percentage concentrated in the basic lowest grade jobs. The design of finance systems to reduce human intervention both reflects these management aims and contributes to them. The Big Four banks in Britain wield enough power as the purchasers of 1 / 6 sophisticated systems to specify to IBM what they want. Lloyds did this 15 years ago when they persuaded IBM UK to develop the earliest European Cashpoint terminals. They also develop a lot of systems in house.

The plain truth is that banks, along with many other sectors of industry, will not require as many highly trained staff as before. Even when business needs dictate, as with professional DP staff, they are still very reluctant to arrange comprehensive training programs. Instead they recruit such qualified specialists from outside, despite the shortage and high salaries that this entails.

Given these conditions, is it appropriate now to argue that training is going to solve all our problems? There will be fewer jobs in banks. If we are to argue for affirmative action programs for women in banks, we have to figure out where those higher jobs are going to come from. We could say that more people should be paid high grades. I'm totally in favor of that. But the employers obviously will not like it, for it is contrary to the entire intention of the way staff profiles are going.

This places women and trade unions in a dilemma. Women's demands for equal opportunities, which increasingly include positive-action programs, are quite rightly reflected in BIFU and other trade union policies. But given the shrinking prospects in the industry, are we raising unrealistic aspirations as to what we as a trade union can achieve?

Are we tacitly accepting that only a very small proportion of our women members will benefit from these programs even if the employers could be persuaded to implement them? The roots of the problem are: (1) diminished employment across the entire population, including the finance industry, and increased unemployment levels; and (2) diminished prospects for higher paid and more satisfying jobs.

Really, I am saying that training is not a panacea. Training is not a cure for those basic problems. These issues must be tackled head-on. They require a government with the political will to intervene in the redistribution of income towards the out-of-work and the badly-paid. Trade unions however have a large contribution to make in pressing for a greatly reduced working week and the creation of more jobs, or at least the retention of current ones. In our union this means maximum agitation for a 28 hour, four-day week, a demand that has been achieved for several small groups of staff.

The Issue of Employment and Office Technology From a Managerial Perspective

John J. Connell
Executive Director
Office Technology Research Group

I was born and brought up in Boston. As one of our great New England poets, Robert Frost, said at one time, "the human brain is a marvelous organism—it starts to work the minute one wakes up in the morning and it doesn't stop until one gets to the office." I start out with this to help make an important point: we are all in this together. The so-called "Office of the Future" is our future, and it's not confined to any one sector of the workforce.

There is now one electronic keyboard terminal for every five office employees in the United States. In five years there will be four for every five. So there is no turning back the tide, and we have to recognize that and live with it.

Secondly, in the current equipment sales picture the fastest area of growth is not in word processors, but in personal computers for the office. These personal computers are not being bought for clerical employees or by clerical employees. They are being bought by managers and professionals for use in their own offices.

When you talk about office machines and electronic technology, then, you are no longer just talking about the clerical workforce. You're talking about everybody who works in an office, all the way up to presidents and chief executive officers. We are all going to be affected, albeit in different ways. So we are all in this boat together.

I grew up in the computer field. For two decades computers were brought into the office for the primary purpose of eliminating clerical jobs. That was the justification for computers from the time they came on the scene in about 1956 almost up to the present. Perhaps that has been less so in the last five years, but in all the payroll departments, the billing departments and the other places where computers were installed, that was the primary purpose of the installation. It worked, too, and we did eliminate a lot of jobs. We also created a lot of jobs.

As a matter of fact, I believe that a study for the Department of Labor on the employment impact of computers over a 20 year period found a net increase in jobs as a result of computers. But the people whose jobs were eliminated did not get the new jobs. If the payroll function was converted to the computer by taking it out of the office and assigning it to the data center, jobs were created for those who wrote the programs and designed the system. However, the new system was run by specialists and no one in the payroll department was made one of those specialists. There were very few job transfers, except perhaps at the data entry level. Therefore the threat of office technology has a history, it has a basis that is real.

But computers aren't going to go away. Our whole economy depends on them. We wouldn't have credit cards if it weren't for computers. Consider the 100-million-share days on the stock market—there's no way one could organize enough office workers in the U.S. to handle that number of shares in a single day. If it weren't for computers this country today would be in absolute financial chaos. With computers, however, we can handle the volume. So they are part of our lives. That doesn't mean that computers have So they are part of our lives. That doesn't mean that computers have to run our lives, but they are a part of our lives.

Starting with word processing in about 1964, office automation came on the scene the same way that computers did. Machine advocates eliminated the secretarial assignment, reorganized the work and tried to put secretaries in a word processing center. We ended up with a lot of unhappy secretaries. But not all of them were unhappy. Some of them realized that this was a new field and jumped on the bandwagon. They got into the word processing field and moved up to supervisory and managerial ranks. Today, a number of them are administrative managers or office systems managers. They started out as secretaries and took advantage of the technology. But for most it was a time of trauma and what caused the trauma was not only dissatisfaction on the part of secretaries, but also the dissatisfaction of the managers when they lost their secretaries.

Economically, word processing is a mixed bag. In the last 15 or 17 years that the technology has been around, one would be hard-pressed to prove that it was really justified economically. The traumas were probably not worth it, but in the process we have learned that the purpose of technology should be the extension of one's capabilities, rather than the elimination of jobs. A manager does not bring a personal computer into his office to get rid of his job. He brings it in as a tool to help him do his job a little better. That attitude is emerging more and more among managers, and it's the personal computer that's causing it more than anything else.

Of course we still have lots of Neanderthal Men in business, as you well know. As far as they are concerned the only reason one brings in a machine is to get rid of a person, to get rid of a job. It's going to take a while to educate people like that. But there are already companies in the U.S. that have adopted internal policies that say: before you introduce machines into the office that affect jobs, you have to identify those people who are affected and come up with comparable or better positions for them, alternative employment opportunities. There are major companies following such rules.

This means that the systems analyst has two jobs. One job is to figure out the new system, and the second is to work with the personnel people to identify alternative and preferably improved employment opportunities.

Finally, I think that what 9to5 and the Working Women Education Fund are doing in terms of educating business is marvelous. But I am concerned about the confrontation philosophy that is coming out of this conference, the feeling that management and office workers have to go head-to-head. I am against the idea of turning to government to try to introduce some sense of order into the question of technology and employment. I think that this group should adopt an advocacy stance, an advocacy that says: if any job in the office is affected by automation, the individual in it has to be offered comparable or better employment.

That will be a selling job. But the pursuit of that advocacy would mean facing up to the fact of technology in a sphere of cooperation and working together, rather than in a confrontation mode. This advocacy would allow one to help people pursue some of the opportunities in the field, and there are tremendous opportunities. So I would like to see such a balanced advocacy: if you eliminate a job, you provide a comparable or better job. And the jobs will be there, perhaps not right now in this recession, but over time, in an information-based economy, the jobs will be there.

The Implications of Technology for U.S. Employment

Roberta McKay
Women's Bureau
U.S. Department of Labor

As a representative of the Women's Bureau, the Federal Agency devoted exclusively to the concerns of women in the labor force, our Director, Dr. Lenora Cole-Alexander, has asked me to express her regrets that she cannot participate in person in this conference on women and new technology.

When we talk about office work and new technology, we are talking principally about jobs women hold, and we are talking about the kind of work most susceptible to the introduction of technologies that incorporate advanced electronics. There is widespread agreement that the pace of diffusion of the new technologies will accelerate over the next few years. Employees and employers should be alerted to these changes taking place and perhaps begin some new policies and comprehensive planning in this area.

We at the Women's Bureau congratulate the Working Women Education Fund and the German Marshall Fund of the U.S. for sponsoring this conference as a means of contributing to such an agenda or "plan of action." We welcome this chance to exchange ideas with our counterparts from abroad and around the country; we want to develop our network of concerned persons with ideas and programs.

I have found that a persistent question concerns the measurement of the effect of technological change on employment, and particularly on the employment of office workers. Economic analysts generally conclude that the impact on employment is not yet clearly discernible. Technology does not happen in isolation; therefore, it is sometimes difficult to quantify while it is happening. Diane Wernecke's study for the International Labour Office found microelectronic technology has not caused widespread displacement of office workers, but perhaps only because poor economic conditions slowed the rate of diffusion.

Rather, when talking about the effect of technological change on office employment, analysts tend to speak in terms of office jobs "affected," rather than eliminated by technological change. For example, a Carnegie-Mellon University study argues that 38 of the 50 million existing white collar jobs will eventually be affected. Xerox Corp. is a little more conservative, saying that with 20 to 30 million will be affected. The fact is employment growth and worker displacement can take place simultaneously. In addition, the impact of technological change on employment may be reflected in a slow-down in employment growth or the use of more part-time workers.

Basic labor force statistics show that a fundamental change in the occupational structure of the work force is taking place in the United States. Laborers and other unskilled workers are becoming a smaller percentage of the labor force. Professional, technical, managerial and service workers are among those increasing at a proportionately greater pace. Higher educational achievement of workers is becoming more the norm.

Today the content of jobs and the qualities required of workers are being modified by technological change. There is less demand for manual dexterity, physical strength for materials handling, and for traditional craftsmanship. In contrast, employers are putting more stress on formal knowledge, precision, and perceptual aptitudes. Microelectronics are being incorporated in systems which control key production equipment such as industrial robots, electronic computers, and numerically controlled machine tools. Moreover, in banks, insurance companies, and retail and wholesale establishments, word processors, computers, data transmission and copying devices, and automatic check-out counters also incorporate microelectronic devices to provide high levels of memory and processing capability.

Advanced technologies in the above industries affect women's employment. Most of the job gains over the last decade have occurred in retail trades, state and local government, and other service industries such as health, business, legal, social, protective, educational, and recreational service.

Although service occupations are expected to increase at the greatest rate, by 1990 the white collar category will experience the largest gain in new jobs—12 to 16 million over the period. Other Bureau of Labor statistics show that women are expected to account for two out of every three new workers. Clerical workers are the largest single white collar occupational catagory, and are expected to increase at a higher rate than average. Women account for eight out of 10 clerical workers. This growth is expected even though computers, word processors, and other office technologies will continue to reduce unit labor requirements, and change skill demands. Professional and technical workers also will continue to be one of the fastest growing occupational catagories. Thus, the trend is towards continued growth in professional/technical occupations and clerical work and a decline in manual, menial and repetitive operative occupations.

Over the 1972-1981 period, the fastest growing occupations in terms of absolute (or numerical) employment increases were:

1. Secretaries
2. Cashiers
3. Registered Nurses
4. Cooks
5. Truckdrivers
6. Accountants
7. Engineers
8. Computer and Peripheral Machine Operators
9. Bookkeepers
10. Computer Specialists

Except for truckdrivers this occupational mix reflects the gains in

white collar and service jobs. The top three gainers, along with computer and peripheral machine operators, are female intensive occupations.
All ten occupations represent 25% of all women employed in wage and
salary jobs compared with about 11% among men. Nonetheless, wom-
en's wages in these jobs are less than their male counterparts and,
except for computer specialists, less than the median salary for the
respective major occupational grouping.

In terms of percentage increase over the 1972-81 period, we see that
computer systems analysts and computer operators are on top. Women
are there, in the leading edge of tomorrow's jobs, but will they continue
to be there?

1.   Computer Systems Analysts
2.   Computer and Peripheral Equipment Operators
3.   Welfare Service Aides
4.   Authors
5.   Psychologists
6.   Research Workers
7.   Economists
8.   Insulation Workers
9.   Teachers Aides
10.   Therapists

Computer analysts and computer and peripheral machine operators
move up from 10th and 7th place in terms of absolute increases, to 1st
and 2nd place. Once again we see the emphasis on a more technically
oriented workforce and higher educational attainment.

Of the two top percentage gainers, though, women dominate the
clerical machine operators, while men dominate the professional systems occupations. This stresses once again the need for women to
obtain counseling on the wide variety of career options and to complete
college and other post secondary education and training programs. It
also points to the need for the retraining of the present workforce. Once
again, male earnings outpace women's. Because these are the emerging
"winners," their share of total employment is much smaller than the old
jobs. But once again, women have the edge; they are somewhat more

into these jobs than men. The question is, how to keep them there and enhance their opportunities in those jobs.

Finally, a look at the leading occupations with declining employment over the 1972-81 period:

1. Delivery and Route Workers
2. Cleaners and Servants in private households
3. Farm Owners and Tenant Farmers
4. Unpaid family farm workers
5. Garage Workers and Gas Station Attendants
6. Sewers and Stitchers (operatives)
7. Child-care workers in private households
8. Textile operatives
9. Telephone operators
10. Stenographers

The occupations posting declines over the period reflect both the movement away from less desirable, dirty and/or low-skilled jobs and the automating of assembly factory operative jobs. Displacement of these workers can add more pressure to the other employment sectors where women have traditionally or historically found employment. Occupational crowding may keep the low wages in these occupations low. In addition, these declines reflect changing life-styles, the demise of family farms and the private household worker.

Declining employment in the textile industry accounted for the single largest share of employment decline among women; for men, it was the decline in farm owners and tenant farmers. The decline in textile employment is a part of the industrial structural realignment in the United States. Nonetheless, it ranks first in women's industrial employment.

Other basic industries undergoing structural changes include the steel and automobile industries, dominated by men. This could mean further pressure on the fragile allocation of the job pie. In other declining female occupations such as telephone operators and stenographers, the earnings are better than average, and the decline can be more closely associated with the word processor, direct-dialing, and other switching devices brought about by the advent of advanced electronics in the workplace.

As the structure of the nation's work force shifts in response to technological innovations and a changing world market for U.S. goods and services, imbalances appear—skill shortage in some sectors, worker displacement in others. Higher educational achievement and training, along with employer and employee job placement flexibility, are becoming more essential and may well determine a worker's future. For some women, perceptions and feelings of occupational isolation and the remaining earnings inequities continue to be problems despite women being on the leading edge of tomorrow's jobs.

References

Leon, Carol Boyd, "Occupation Winners and Losers: Who They were During 1972-80," **Monthly Labor Review,** June 1982, U. S. Department of Labor, Bureau of Labor Statistics.

Levitan, S.A. and C.M Johnson, "The Future of Work: Does it Belong to Us or to the Robots?" **Monthly Labor Review,** September 1982, U. S. Department of Labor, Bureau of Labor Statistics.

Norwood, Janet L. **The Female-Male Earnings Gap: A Review of Employment and Earnings Issues,** U. S. Department of Labor, Bureau of Labor Statistics.

Riche, Richard W., speech, "Impact of Technological Change" for the OECD's Second Special Session on Information Technology, Productivity, Working Conditions and Employment, Paris, France, October 19-21, 1981 and **Monthly Labor Review,** March 1982, U. S. Department of Labor, Bureau of Labor Statistics.

U. S. Department of Labor, Office of the Secretary, Women's Bureau, **Equal Employment Opportunity for Women: U. S. Policies.** United States Report for the Organization for Economic Cooperation and Development (OECD), Working Party Number 6 on the Role of Women in the Economy, Paris, France, June 1982.

Werneke, Diane, **Microelectronics and Office Jobs: The Impact of the Chip on Women's Employment,** report prepared for the International Labour Office, 1982.

Working Women Education Fund, **Race Against Time: Automation of the Office,** 1980, Cleveland, Ohio.

Assessing the Myths
of the Job Market

Joan Greenbaum
Professor of Data Processing
LaGuardia Community College

I would like to talk about the myths of the job market, specifically those myths related to technology. In addition to being a teacher of data processing, I'm an economist. The first question that needs to be asked is: Will technology create more jobs? My answer is a clear "No." If you look at how technology is being used in the production sector, in factories, you will see that it is responsible for the loss of a great number of jobs. In the last few years, some 1.2 million factory jobs have been lost, a large chunk directly related to technology. There is no question that technology in factory jobs is introduced as "labor saving," or, as the British call it, "head-chopping."

Will technology be used differently in offices? I think the answer again is clearly "No." We are not creating more jobs. We are getting rid of workers.

In response a counter argument is often put forward that says, well, it will replace some workers, but new categories will be created. This is a false argument. There have been approximately 20,000 new computer programmer jobs created every year in the last couple of years. But 20,000 jobs is not very many at all. Sure, there has been an increase in 250,000 computer operation jobs in the last half decade, but computer operators are increasingly marginalized, made more part-time, given lower salaries, and at this point are majority women.

So that's the first myth, that technology in the office of the future will create more jobs. I say absolutely "No." The thing that creates more jobs is job creation programs, not technology.

The second myth: will the jobs that do come into existence with new technology be better? Will they require more skill, more integration of tasks, and involve more enjoyable work circumstances? My answer is again: "No, not necessarily." There's no magic that says the technology by itself will make these jobs more interesting. In the factory sector, dull and boring jobs have been automated, but they haven't been replaced with exciting jobs. We have heard about the integration of tasks through the use of micro-computers and personal computers, but that has to do with middle-management positions, not clerical positions.

Well, what about jobs in high technology? We hear a lot about jobs in high technology. Are they growing very rapidly? I think we have to be careful when we cite statistics from the Bureau of Labor Statistics (BLS). They use two different numbers. They say jobs in the computer field are growing most rapidly. Absolutely true, they are. But they are growing the fastest from a very tiny base. They are talking about the rate of growth. Computer programming, for example, has doubled in the last decade. But there are only 350,000 to 400,000 people in that occupation category. That's trivial compared to the number of people in any major state that have been laid off in the last year or so. It's a drop in the bucket.

You also hear that "high-tech" jobs are growing. Those are assembly jobs. They are the lowest wage, the most part-time, and almost completely women. And they increasingly are farmed out to what are modern day sweatshops at minimum wage or slightly above. We can call these "high-tech" because they are people assembling micro-electronic chips. But it ain't glamorous. So we have to be careful of labels like "high-tech" and "fastest growing field" because they are lumping a lot of things into those categories.

So what jobs are growing the most in numbers? For the decade of the 1970s the categories that did grow were led by secretaries, some 900,000 plus. And cashiers. Is that a high-paying job? Cooks. By cooks, however, they don't mean chefs, they mean workers in marginalized, part-time McDonalds and fast food restaurants. We are not talking about high level skills here. Another fast growing category is bank tellers, but again these are comparatively low-paying jobs, and are increasingly part-time.

For the most part these are jobs that can be divided up so that they can be made part-time, and possibly into homework; they can be farmed out in little pieces to individuals doing work at home instead of people working collectively together in offices.

There is a rather interesting statistic about growth in any occupational category in the last few years. I looked at the median wages for women for all growing job categories, including all in the professional categories, and there is not a single women's occupational category in which the women's median wage would support the median wage for a family of four in 1981 statistics. That includes doctors and lawyers, by the way, and includes the median wage for computer programmers. There was no data available for engineers.

So what do we do about this? I would argue that it must be approached through some form of association or union organizing. And we have to talk about unions that are different from unions in the past. Industrial unionism grew up on the basis that a factory was a single location, and that management invested a lot of capital and equipment in that one place. Workers were face to face, and union organizing meant that you could bargain collectively around a series of issues pertaining to that location.

What do we see with new technology? We see that it's decreasing in cost very rapidly, and increasing the mobility of capital. Management will be able to move offices almost wherever they want to. They can move offices into people's homes, or make work more part-time. No longer can we use the example of an industrial union that is just in one location. We have to talk about community-oriented demands that say: "We need open career ladders."

Robyn Dasey from Great Britain raised the issue of retraining. I agree with her perspective. You can't talk about retraining unless you talk about some fundamental issues. What are the jobs? Can we create meaningful career ladders? Can we create paths so that people can advance as positions are opened up?

We also have to be careful about the argument that we need a lot of technical specialists. Particularly in the community college where I teach, we have begun to talk about the return of liberal arts education. We need to talk about critical thought skills, so that people are aware that the job market is in fact very limited and limiting if they get wedged into one of these narrow technical sub-specialties.

Engineering, for instance, which is supposed to be a great growth field, has 85 sub-specialties according to the BLS. So if one of your children decides to enter college and study engineering in one of these 85 sub-specialties, who is to say that the one in 85 will be in demand five or six years from now? It's like a game of Russian roulette.

In conclusion, we need to demand career ladders, open training and more broad-based training that we don't pay the cost of. We can't keep taking the guilt, the blame, that my job has changed and therefore I must retrain myself. We must beware of the myths of the job market and say: more jobs, better jobs, through technology.

Productivity and Service Quality in the Private Sector

Michael Hammer
Hammer & Company
Department of Electrical Engineering
and Computer Science
Massachusetts Institute of Technology

My background is as an engineer. Most of my activities today are working with management to make effective use of new technology. I suppose I would consider myself a friendly critic of the technology and the people who try to use it. To put it bluntly, my perspective is that I do not view cost reduction and labor displacement as morally objectionable. That's part of the objective that people are looking for. But in fact, this is rarely accomplished using the new office technologies.

So let me talk about the private sector. The term generally used at this conference has been the "service industries," but I prefer to think of these more as service functions, because even in so-called manufacturing industries there are a lot of service functions such as customer service.

I've done a lot of work with the users of office systems, and I've seen a phenomenon that I call the "neo-Parkinson effect." This stems from Parkinson's Law: that work expands to fill the amount of time available for it. With new technologies we find that work expands to fill the amount of equipment available for it.

For example, I spoke to the managing partner of a large New York law firm. They have word processors as far as you can see, yet they still have the same ratio of secretaries to attorneys that you have in a non-automated law firm. So I asked: "How did you get by in the old days? What did you have, 10,000 typists?" He said: "No, in the old days briefs went through three drafts, not forty." I said: "Are forty drafts better than three?" He answered: "I have no idea, but you give attorneys the opportunity, and they will polish their approach till the sky falls."

I'm familiar with companies that make extensive use of electronic mail, which is supposed to displace internal mail systems and the telephone. A number of managers in those companies are terribly resistant to its use because they find that there is no disincentive for anybody to communicate with them; they spend much more time pawing through electronic junk mail than they ever did sorting through the paper mail that comes across their desk.

This is a terrible syndrome that perhaps started with the copying machine. Market research for the copying machine indicated that there was no market for the convenient copier. It did not address an existing need. It did not displace existing equipment. Rather, it was a technology that created its own demand.

Sad to say, not only are demands for services insatiable, but people's desires seem to be infinite. If you give people the opportunity to use technology to generate more work, they will do that even if the work has no intrinsic business value. So there is so-called cost reduction that is not cost-reduction. It is cost avoidance. We do ten times the amount of work, but it doesn't cost us any more, or maybe it only costs us twice as much, and so the vendors of the equipment try to convince us that we are better off. Well, in fact, we are spending twice as much for getting ten times as much paper.

In fact, the office is not a factory. This is obvious, but let me tell you what I mean. Productivity is not a word that means happy or successful or profitable or Japanese. It means output per unit of input, or per unit of labor, or per unit of capital. It presumes the ability to effectively measure output. But most offices do not have output of intrinsic economic value. Having twice as many meetings or twice as many memoranda or twice as many reports... is that twice as good? Sometimes it's twice as good. Sometimes it's twice as bad. Usually it's twice as irrelevant. Setting up the use of technology as producing more paper is fundamentally sterile, a waste of money from management's point of view. So in fact, what you have to look at is not efficiency. Efficiency is a misleading term in most offices.

Of course, there are some offices that are, in fact, factories: order entry offices, or insurance claims processing, or check processing in banks. But those offices already have been highly automated for a long time. The offices we are looking at today are places where we get jobs done. Here the issue is not efficiency, it is effectiveness. What's the difference? Efficiency is doing the thing the right way. While effectiveness is doing the right thing. If I am not being effective, efficiency is of no value to me. If I am driving off a cliff, I would rather go ten miles an hour than 80 miles an hour.

In use and service organizations, the objective of new technology is to improve the quality of service. In an insurance company, for example, this means the ability to respond to inquiries more quickly, to achieve a lower error rate, to identify new opportunities, to be innovative, to introduce new products at a faster rate. And none of these are measured in tangible, paper-oriented terms. This is not to say that they are fluffy and fuzzy areas; they are real business benefits. But they are not "productivity" as such.

In fact, when people start talking to me about managerial and professional productivity, I get very nervous. I am always reminded of what Dorothy Parker said when they told her that Calvin Coolidge had died. She said: "How can you tell?" And when somebody tells me they have improved managerial productivity, I want to know how they know. What's their measure? Billions of insights per fortnight? In fact, it's how well the business is getting its job done.

Let me wrap up. What are the impacts on employment? The net impact of new technologies, when employed effectively, is in fact to create employment. Now perhaps I am being optimistic in this regard. If the demand in the public sector for services is infinite, so is the demand of private sector companies to be more competitive. The real potential of new technology is that it enables private sector companies to stop spending their time worrying about paperwork—the last thing in the world they care about—and to start thinking about being more aggressive in the marketplace by introducing new products and servicing customers more effectively.

In the last five or six years, there has been a lot of implementation of automated systems in banks. One particular area is letter of credit. The effect has been a net improvement in the quality of service rendered to the bank's corporate customers with no decrease in employment, although there has been an important change in employment. The people who formerly had been working in clerical tasks now have para- or even fully professional jobs working essentially as accounts representatives. The computer machine is doing the routine paper handling.

A fundamental part of any service business is the quality of human relationships, and the machine will never address this. But as the machine can deal with the paperwork more effectively, the people get to do more of the people-work. And this capacity, fundamentally, is what is required in the private-sector service area in order to be more competitive.

III. Effects on the Quality and Organization of Work

Automation and the Quality of Work Life at the Swedish Telephone Company:
A Management View

Brita Tornqvist & Svea Hermansson
Svensk Televerket, Sweden

The Swedish Telecommunications Administration (Televerket) is a state-owned commercial enterprise, directed by the Ministry of Communications, with a monopoly on the operation of the Swedish telecommunications network. Televerket is required to deliver some surplus to the Public Treasury.

The object of Televerket is to give comparable service to all subscribers wherever they live, whether in towns or in the countryside.

In the last ten years a number of factors have increased Televerket's costs. It has met competition from private companies selling new electronic equipment, mobile radiocommunication systems, data equipment, and other services which may be connected to the telephone network. At the same time, salaries have increased significantly. The manual services have been very expensive.

For this reason Televerket last year began to charge for certain directory services that formerly were free of charge, e.g. when somebody asks for the name and address of a subscriber to a certain number. (This is considered to be an exclusive service and is not available in all countries. When you ask for the number of a certain subscriber, the directory inquiries service is still free of charge.)

The charge was not sufficient to give a surplus, however, so Telever-ket looked to other methods to increase production. Every manual service was expected to bear its own expenses. The first effort was to introduce data equipment to replace the manual handling of paper files, telephone directories, etc.

Union/Management Working Groups

It was at that stage that the union was involved. The information section in Stockholm where Svea Hermansson is the manager was the first section in Televerket where they tried to adapt both localities and positions to the operators' work with data equipment. We had been working for some years with comfiche but the operators did not like it. The figures and letters were difficult to read and the light on the screen was not good.

Televerket calculated on cutting down on the costs by about 20% through higher productivity and by reducing the manual work of cor-recting and inserting new data in the files.

What was the economic result?

Reduced costs of operators	20%
Reduced operating time	8%
Reduced number of positions	15%

The annual cost of the Automated Data Processing (ADP) system turns out to be lower than the cost of the previous manual handling of the files. Paper costs continue rising while data costs are decreasing.

The unions were engaged in working groups. Svea Hermansson was working for the union at that time to make the environment as good as possible for the operators.

As visual displays were introduced in the interception service, a joint working group was formed, with representatives of the unions and of Televerket.

We started working out specifications of the requirements for differ-ent functions, such as the height of the tables, lighting, the placing of displays, etc. To get the best possible result we engaged an ergonomist and an architect. Then we started to work with great intensity together with the consultants we had engaged.

In order to analyze alternative operators' positions, we made study visits to various offices where positions different from the traditional ones were used. We also had to consider the localities. The position we decided upon was built up in the old operating room to give the staff a chance to try it.

We did the same thing with the keyboard, the suspension device of the display, the qualities of the table (surface, microphone sockets and the "vertically adjustable" function). Lighting, an important factor in VDT work, was arranged with the help of an ergonomist. The architect and the ergonomist were consulted regarding the colouring of the room and positions, curtains and carpets.

All the time during the work the personnel was kept informed and could influence the work of the group. (What could not be changed were the details worked out with the ergonomist.)

When everything was ready for occupation, we thought the result was very nice to look at. But nothing is so good that it can't be better, so we keep making improvements when necessary.

In addition to the reduced costs, we achieved several improvements both for the customers and for the operators.

- Better and more detailed information to the customers
- Easier charging through a minicomputer connected to the data system and to the billing system
- Better working environment for the operators such as: more space for each operator and less noise in the room.

In addition, the positions are ergonomically designed and flexible for use by both left- and right-handed persons; the data equipment is adapted to the operator with the screen and keyboard adjustable in all directions; and the lighting in the room is specially made to fit screen work by neutralizing reflections and dazzling effects.

Minimizing The Negative Effects

In the "paper age" the operators had been working in big, unhealthy rooms, sitting close together in a noisy stressful environment. The working group had to improve everything.

After introducing the new techniques, interviews were made with the operators to evaluate their feelings in contrast to the former techniques. And investigations were made concerning the ergonomical and psychological aspects.

Dr. Eva Gunnarsson at the Swedish Working Life Center has made an investigation described in the report: **Eye-Strain resulting from VDT Work at the Swedish Telecommunications Administration.** She found that when the VDT work routines are intensified, the symptoms of visual strain will increase more among employees above the age of 40 than among those below 35. 13-20% had problems with visual strain, headache and visual fatigue. Therefore all operators received eye-glasses, intended for looking at the screen, after examination by an optician.

As a result of union demands, Televerket has tried job rotation. The operators sit for only two hours at the data equipment and then change to other types of work, with paper files or administrative work, and eventually come back for another 2 hours' work with data terminals.

This can be done by a schedule. We inserted in the schedule two hours on the day shift, working with the data equipment. So the operator knows from the beginning of the shift in what section she will be working. How should we know at what time she should work at the data equipment or in other sections? We made some measurements of the traffic, the number of the calls, in every section for every hour. The measurements are made *only* of the of the group, never of individuals. We make measurements for the whole group of data equipment service and information service, and then we know hour by hour how many operators have to work in that hour. So the operators themselves make a schedule. No supervisors tell them. When they come to the job, they look at the schedule and say: "I will sit there, and I will sit there..." And there you have a job rotation.

Survey Results

The result of an inquiry with 116 operators after the installation of data equipment was that 95.7% found it easier and better to work with data terminals than with paper and directories. The reasons were: less strain on arms and shoulders, no heavy books to lift, faster and more detailed information, better total environment, etc.

The negative effects were visual strain, headache, etc.; reflections, wrong colour on the screen background and the letters; dazzling effects, static electricity, etc. It was irritating too when the computer broke down and you had to wait for an answer from the computer memory. The short average operating time, 35 seconds, makes the work intensive and causes visual strains. To get rid of that, we have to have more breaks than before, now 15 minutes after every two hours, and have instituted gym breaks once a day; there are also information and productivity group meetings for solving working problems and making proposals for better working methods and environment. It's not the most difficult thing to improve all these negative effects.

In conclusion, we have found that the training must be flexible to make it possible to handle several kinds of tele-services in the same data terminal in the future. Information about the whole chain of data work and routines for every type of service, and about how the information is input into the ADP system, are necessary ingredients.

The physical and ergonomical aspects of the working environment have been well looked after, but the psychological aspects, the necessity of avoiding routines too simple and monotonous, have been neglected. Job rotation or integration of different services are possible solutions. The fear of losing one's job and the need for meaningful work are problems that must be solved by both the unions and Televerket.

Automation and the
Quality of Work Life
at the
Swedish Telephone Company
A Union View

Berith Westman
ST-Televerket, Sweden

In my speech I will concentrate on four points:

I   Brief description of the working routines at a sales department before computerization and after

II   Positive and negative effects of computerization

III   Problems today, and maybe tomorrow, as a result of computerization

IV   What demands we make on the employer in connection with computerization, and the agreements we have concluded with the Swedish Telecommunications Administration, called Televerket.

I. Handling Customer Requests

I. I will start by describing the work at a sales department. It consists mainly in dealing with matters related to customer calls, such as orders for new subscriptions, removal of telephones, or transfers of subscriptions. Before computerization there were customer card files. When a telephone removal was ordered, the order was written on a special form which was then typed out with a number of copies and checked. Then it was forwarded to the dispatching department and other departments concerned.

Today the work is computerized. When the customer calls Televerket to have his telephone removed, the operator keys the subscriber number which appears on the display and records the commission, which then is forwarded to the dispatching department.

With computerization, 14 working elements have been replaced by two at the sales department.

The work at the sales department after computerization may be described as VDT work, periodically intensive and sometimes interspersed with other tasks.

II. Positive and Negative Effects

II. What is felt to be a positive effect by the employees is that orders are handled faster thanks to simplified routines. The information to customers is more easily available.

In some departments the staff have integrated the display work with other manual tasks and so broadened their knowledge. This is felt to be a great advantage.

Computerization has also had negative effects, especially the fact that working routines are increasingly controlled by the computer. The information on the screen and the sequence of the pictures guide the conversation with customers. But the control also means that you are totally stranded by a computer breakdown. Then you can't do anything as you have no influence on the computer. Breakdowns in the computer system are felt by most employees to be very irritating and stressful.

At the sales department it is today harder to follow the development of a commission. Earlier the "history" of a subscription was noted on a card - today the information is stored only for a short period in the computer.

The most negative effect of computerization today is felt to be the imposed inactivity. The pace and amount of work vary a great deal from day to day. On days when orders are few and the employees have not managed to integrate their work with other tasks, there is very little to do.

III. Employment and Training

The really big problem from the union's point of view is above all employment. Computerization has led to a situation where Televerket needs fewer employees. So far no one has been dismissed as there were vacancies to be filled. A prevalent view also has been that the present and future problem with supernumerary staff would be solved by a sufficient number of retirements.

Televerket is an enterprise expanding its activities into new areas, such as office automation. This puts us as a staff organization at Televerket in a rather awkward situation. We want Televerket to succeed in this new field, as it is important for the employees to keep their jobs. At the same time, Televerket has clearly stated that the employees are expected to act as guinea pigs in relation to its products, such as Teletex.

A success for Televerket in this field means that certain tasks will disappear, to be replaced by others. The problem is that those who once did the work that now disappears lack the training needed for the new tasks. As a union we must insist on the employer applying a substantial time margin in his staff planning—and make sure that he does!—and on the employees being trained to be able to cope with their new tasks.

We know that it is mainly women's jobs that will disappear. As women we must therefore support each other and inspire each other with courage and self-confidence. We must insist on training and seek the training available that is needed for more qualified work. Otherwise we will be replaced by well-educated man, recruited from outside Televerket.

Another important problem is the content of work. As far as we know, computerization has undermined the content of work, especially with respect to work already considered to be monotonous. As a union counter-measure we have pushed our demand that no employee should be forced to sit at the terminal for more than two hours. So far we have managed pretty well, but we have no guarantees for the future. Today it is possible to intersperse terminal work with other, manual tasks, but the present trend points to more tasks being computerized until finally there may be no manual work left.

IV. A Question of Power

Finally, I wish to mention our union's demands on the employer in connection with computerization and the agreements we have concluded with Televerket.

As a union we can after all find many constructive aspects of the new technique. Therefore, the union fight is not directed against the new technique, against the computers, robots or office automation equipment as such. It is fought against the negative effects of the technique. The following requirements must be satisfied to avoid changes for the worse:

- guaranteed job security for all employees
- changes in work organization so as to achieve a local distribution of tasks and to reduce the disintegration and breaking up of the work
- intensive routine work at the terminal shall be limited to two hours a day per person

The role played by the ADP technique is not mainly a technical matter, but a question of power. It is a question of who will be able to carry through his demands.

The knowledge, unity, fighting spirit and sense of responsibility of our members will determine our influence. The absolute condition for our acceptance of the new technique is that we have enough influence to carry through our principal demands.

It is not possible to develop a well-functioning data system in the face of opposition by the personnel that is to operate the system. For this reason, rationalization of work, in order to be efficient, must be based on a mutual understanding between employers and unions about the working conditions. This understanding shall be negotiated and settled in agreements.

Televerket and the staff organizations have concluded one rationalization agreement and one ADP agreement.

The ADP agreement indicates the direction and basic principles to be followed in connection with the introduction of ADP aids of all kinds, from word/text processors to large computers.

According to the agreement, computerization shall be introduced with a view to profitability, taking into account employees' requirements for a good working environment, opportunities for advancement, and co-determination. As regards system structure, the aim shall be to obtain systems promoting the established organization philosophy with respect to delegation of authority and decentralization. This means that in connection with systems development, local or highly distributed solutions shall be selected on a preferential basis.

The agreement also stipulates that for all types of computerization the aim shall be to seek systems solutions designed so as to give the users of the system comprehensive and varied tasks. The terminal work shall be organized and the positions designed so as to create a good working environment.

There is a clause in the agreement prescribing that computerization shall be carried out without personnel being dismissed or being forced to move from one town to another.

In summary, I want to emphasize the importance of the union taking part in the early period of the planning for the new technology and the new methods of the work.

New Technology and Its Implications in U.S. Clerical Work

Roslyn Feldberg and Evelyn N. Glenn
Boston University

In our work we have tried to get close to what is actually going on in offices. What we will discuss is what we see as some of the trends in the the United States in a few of the offices we have examined in some detail. We also will provide a couple of examples of some of the contradictory implications and consequences of the way in which office technology is being used. Finally, we will raise some questions about possible implications that need to be taken into careful consideration.

At the outset let's be very clear about the differences between the American and the European context. There are no legally-mandated standards in the U.S. for the use of equipment, nor are there enforced regulations about kinds of equipment. We also have no legislation that mandates worker or union participation in decisions about the introduction and use of technology. And in the U.S. a very, very small proportion of clerical workers are unionized or organized into employee associations of any kind. The result is that we are operating in a very different context.

When we began looking at office automation and the debate over the coming of office automation, as it was called in the early '70s, it was quickly brought to our attention that there were two different schools of thought.

One group of people said that office automation was going to be good for everyone; I leave you to guess which group this was. The other group said it was going to be bad for everyone. As Harley Shaiken has pointed out, the effects of office automation, both good and bad, tend to differ depending on which group you are talking about. We have found that the effects are very different, not only in the sense of what's happening for management, for productivity and for the quality of work life, but also within the offices, for different groups within the clerical labor force.

First, a quick overview of the study. (This research was supported by National Institute of Mental Health Grant MH-30932.) It is based on two large organizations, one an insurance company and the other a utility. About 85% of the workers in the insurance company do clerical work, as do 25% in the utility. We observed people in the workplace, interviewed about 178 workers, and talked to workers and managers informally.

We had expected to find that some of the negative effects were spreading throughout clerical jobs. The most evident negative effects in the early stages of automation were those associated with key-punching: monotony and being tied to a desk and to an activity of one particular kind. We actually found a somewhat more complex picture. There is evidence of de-skilling in many areas. There is also evidence of a loss of opportunities for mobility and the loss of relationships in certain areas. But the effects take place at different rates and in different ways in different areas of the clerical labor force. In other words, we observed contradictory effects of automation on job skills. Some formerly skilled jobs are clearly deskilled, while in other jobs the deskilling is not so clear, with some jobs coming to involve a wider range of knowledge and autonomy.

There has also been a major change in the organization of office work: a new layer has been added to the office hierarchy. In previous decades there were clerical workers and managers in the largely clerical industries. Now a new group has been added, the technical personnel, and it is making a big difference. The new set of technical jobs is becoming very important in shaping the organization of office work and the hierarchies in the office. The expansion in computer specialists jobs has been used to point to supposed new opportunities for mobility into skilled jobs as computer operators, programmers and analysts. However, these jobs are inaccessible to lower level clerical workers who are displaced by automation. The higher level technical jobs require formal credentials; so new groups of specialists with formal credentials get recruited from outside the company. Thus one can say that new skilled jobs are created by automation, yet this does not necessarily increase channels of mobility for those already employed in the office. Instead, this new stratification reinforces the trend toward credentialism which has accelerated in the past 20 years (for example, access to lower level management jobs through job experience has become more difficult because formal educational requirements have been adopted.)

At present the specialist jobs are very separate from clerical jobs, and it's an empirical question whether and in what ways they will become more closely integrated. Will these new jobs become part of a structure that provides clerical workers with new job opportunities? So far that does not seem to be the case in the U.S.

As to the clerical jobs themselves, instead of finding that they have become more homogeneous, we found new dimensions of stratification based on different kinds of technical skills, and new forms of stratification related to the use of new technology in supervision.

We found that four major kinds of clerical work seem to be emerging out of hundreds of job titles. The first is secretarial work, although the nature of that work is changing. The second distinct type is what we call "all-around" work. These clerks do all of the different phases of a job, a complete job, as opposed to a particular sub-activity. The third type is "coding" done by clerks who translate various kinds of information from text into codes which can then be entered into the computer. And the fourth type is data entry in which clerks called data entry operators do the actual entry work.

What is beginning to happen with these jobs is that they are undergoing varying forms of rationalization. One form of rationalization is more exact job descriptions—attempts by management to say more specifically what the work is supposed to be and how the workers are supposed to do it. We found separate career ladders for the different major specialties—secretaries, all-around clerks, coding clerks, and data entry. The job ladders are limited—they have few rungs, perhaps three or four levels—but the route is very clear: one has to come in at the bottom and move slowly up the ranks. A second form is more limited training—being taught to do only the required tasks narrowly defined. (A third form is more finely sub-divided tasks in some jobs.)

Women with different social characterisitics seem to get recruited for the different specialties; movement from one specialty to another is very rare. Because of the special job ladders, previous experience is not essential for the jobs involving entry, coding or other tasks closely related to data processing. The companies prefer women without experience to train because the format of the system (e.g. control buttons) are specific to the company. Previous experience on a different system is thought to interfere because it takes time to unlearn. The feeling is that data entry and coding can be taught in a few hours, especially since the training involves only knowledge needed to do a particular job, rather than providing an overall view of the system.

Here's a brief example of the implications of these changes. Data entry is the area of clerical work that seems to be the most rationalized, in which the de-skilling is most obvious. In an earlier period, key-punchers had to know how to program their machines, that is how to set up up the fields for entering information. This is now done by the technical staff, and data entry operators are not trained for this work. According to managers of data entry departments, data entry operators are only taught which buttons to press for the format, then they type in the information. They are not expected to decide whether or not the information they type is correct; that decision is made by an internal computer check.

In fact, it is not that simple. People complain that their training is inadequate, and that they can't do their jobs well because they don't understand their equipment well enough. When we interviewed people on the job, and asked them to explain to us what they did, they would say: "Talk to so-and-so because I've only been on the job for eight months." Implicitly, they recognized that with experience people doing their jobs do develop specific knowledge and skills. In fact they figure out the content of meaningless codes, and develop the ability to decide whether a serious error has been made. They learn a lot more than management expects them to know or gives them credit for knowing.

But these unrecognized skills are not credentialed in any way. They are not part of workers' job descriptions, and therefore cannot be the basis for moving into a job that depends on having those skills. If workers don't "officially" have the skills, it is difficult for them to prove they do have them. There is no structure for assessing and acknowledging skills gained on-the-job, although occasionally workers do succeed in gaining recognition for their skills.

As an example of some of the problems that changing work organization creates for the quality of work life, let's look at a job that is seen as becoming more integrated and "improved." This job, known as customer representative or telephone representative, consists of answering the phone when a customer or client calls with a complaint or question. Most large companies are developing large numbers of these jobs, said to be the "best" clerical jobs in these organizations. The customer representatives usually sit with VDT terminals in front of them; they have access to the central data bank; they can call up your account, and they are supposed to be able to answer questions you might have on billing and other business matters. They have broad, general training, learn a lot about company policies, and they are given a bit of discretion in negotiating with customers.

One of the effects of this new integrated job is that customer representatives hear all the complaints from customers. They experience the tension of dealing with and trying to defuse people's dissatisfaction with the company's policies. Yet there is little they can do in response to these complaints. Why? They have limited authority to make decisions, and, second, they work on a machine-paced system—calls are automatically distributed to open lines— on which they are closely monitored for quality control and productivity. They cannot take care of your problem if it's going to take too long and interfere with their record at the end of the day. Moreover, because the worker is tied to the desk—she doesn't have to get up to look at files in different departments—she is subject to more visual supervision and control. The way the job has been structured therefore increases external surveillance and managerial control, and the experience of the work may be that there is less autonomy, even though the range of the job has widened.

Unlike the Swedish system, where records are kept by department, in American offices the new technology is often used to keep individual records. Each worker is responsible for his or her own productivity. The result is a very demanding pace of work and a close system of monitoring and productivity checks. Supervisors can tell whether the worker is answering the phone, if any callers have hung up while waiting to be served, and so on; all that information is immediately available to them. And, of course, they can listen in on the line.

We also observed that tasks can be sufficiently simplified or "automated" so that they can be recombined in different ways, among different employees, at different stages of the automating process. Deskilling can occur as a process with different impacts at different stages of automation. For example, as data entry formats are pre-programmed, entry is speeded up and simplified. Similarly with coding, jobs created by computerization involve less decision-making and interpretation in more advanced systems because coding procedures are more elaborate and carefully specified.

As systems get increasingly sophisticated, there is now a trend toward decentralization of these specialized coding and data entry tasks, so that these tasks can be combined either together or as part of jobs performed by other workers. When pre-programmed VDT instructions for entry are printed on the screen, the operator needs only know how to sign on. Thus entry can be done by anyone at the point at which the data is generated, for example by secretaries at the hospital where the claims originate. The insurance company is trying to move toward entry at the point of origin by persons generating the data, thus reducing the need for a specialized bank of data entry operators. Similarly, there is a trend in the utility company to simplify coding and data entry by having departments record everything on precoded data forms. Simplified coding and entry can be added to other jobs, for example telephone inquiry clerks are now required to do entry work during slack hours.

Finally, let us mention the broader implications. As a result of changes associated with the new technology, decisions about how work is to be organized are being made further and further away from the actual users of the technology. We have been in offices where people walk into work on Friday morning and find memos on their desks saying that a new system will be in place on Monday morning. These systems don't necessarily work, and the workers are not given enough information about the new technology to enter the discussion of how these systems should be designed.

In addition, the pressure for productivity leads to tension on the job, and problems in doing a quality of work that is satisfying to the workers. Even if other aspects of the work are acceptable, productivity pressures may interfere with a meaningful quality of work on the job.

Finally there's the empirical question of the extent to which there will be a loss of employment as a result of some of these changes. A lot of this loss seems to be hidden. There's attrition as opposed to actual announced ending of jobs. Some jobs are made part-time, and part-time workers are less visible when their numbers are reduced. So there are many unanswered questions about the long-term implications—in terms of workers' abilities to develop skills, to have opportunities to improve their situations on the job, and to have jobs at all—of the way this technology is being used.

The Role of Common Sense in the Process of Interface Design

Lucy Suchman
Xerox Palo Alto Research Center

For several years now I have been very interested in the kinds of theories about work that guide the design of new technology. When I say "theories" I am not talking so much about the attempts to achieve some kind of "science of human factors" as I am talking about what are best thought of as folk theories. That is, the kind of commonly held accounts of the world and human behavior that we all rely on from day to day.

Some of these folk theories are very general, that is, they are accounts that we all share simply in virtue of our membership in the society at large. Some of them are more specialized, and come out of our participation in a particular community. Together, they make up what we think of as our common sense. "Common" because it is shared in virtue of our membership in some general or special community; and "sense" in that it represents the notions that we have about the nature and significance of every-day situations and events.

As members of this society in general and the design community in particular, designers (I'm using this term very broadly and with some poetic license) rely on their common sense. That is, like everyone else, they bring to their work a lot of assumptions about the world, about human behavior, and especially about the work for which they are designing. This use of common sense as a resource is sometimes touted in the design community as the "art" of design, and sometimes bemoaned as the absence of "science." In fact I think it is both. I think the role of common sense in interface design is a double-edged sword, and it's the two edges of that sword that I want to talk about today.

The first edge is a concern that I have, which has to do with the use of common sense as a resource in design. My concern is that the kinds of folk theories that common sense provides may effectively ensure that new technologies simply perpetuate old misconceptions. The second edge of the sword is a hope that I have about common sense as a subject. The hope is that, as a subject that we adequately understand, common sense might lead to genuine innovations in design that would actually lend some substance to the so far largely empty talk about "friendly" systems.

To illustrate my concern, let me briefly describe two studies that I have done. One study concerned office work, that is, ordinary procedural clerical work. The other was of machine operation, specifically the use of an ordinary, everyday photocopier. These two fairly mundane investigations gave me a glimpse into the ways in which common sense assumptions about these two domains of work might slow the progress of real innovation in the design of new technologies.

First, the office. A prevailing folk theory of office work since Taylorism is that the structure of the work is, or should be, a reflection of procedural specifications. Several years ago I did a fairly concentrated observational study of what goes on in offices, and I made the following not very surprising observation. People don't actually carry out procedures. That is, the work that people do is not the same as the execution of a step-wise sequence of instructions. That observation is not surprising because anyone who has spent any time at all in an office knows that what people actually do is not identical with the procedural specifications. In deference to the theory of how office work should operate, people usually report their experiences of this fact either in the form of apologies, or complaints to the effect that, while the procedures sound nice, to the extent that they fail to really take into account the complexity of the actual cases (which is very much indeed), they don't actually tell you what to do.

Given this common experience, what are we to make of the persistence of this folk theory that office work should be describable as a compendium of procedures? One way to understand it would be to say that this is just one more case where practice falls short of theory. That is, as a consequence of a messy and imperfect world, the actual practice of office work is a sort of faulty approximation of the ideal.

The approach that shed some light on this question for me, however, was just the opposite. When I let go of this common sense idea, that what actually goes on in offices is a failed attempt at doing things according to procedure, everything became much more comprehensible. Specifically, the work is about handling cases in a way that is accountable to organizational policies and procedures. But the cases themselves are real-world events and, as such, they are not organized procedurally. So office work is about making non-procedural events accountable to administrative procedures. The procedures, of course, are not instructions for doing that work, at least not in the way that we commonly think of instructions. They don't actually tell you what to do, but they do give you the grounds for judging whether a fit can be made between the events and the framework that the procedures provide. Learning that process of adjudication, its terms and its boundaries, is what the work, and the skill of doing it, are all about.

I found something surprisingly similar when I looked at machine operation. Again the issue was instructions: what they are in their ordinary, everyday form and what it means to follow them. In this case I looked at first-time users of a copier that was intended by its designers (or actually by its marketers, an important distinction) to be self-explanatory. You were supposed to be able to walk up to the machine and figure out how to use it just on the basis of the information that was there, in and on the machine. Reports from users indicated that in fact this didn't work. For some reason this machine actually was quite difficult to figure out.

Our common-sense assumption about this task is that it is essentially a task of following instructions, and that the difficulties that people encounter in doing it must be the result of bad instructions, of which there certainly are many examples in the world, or stupid users, of which I think there are fewer examples. Here again I found that if I abandoned this notion that the trouble is the result of the instructions not being quite good enough, the failure of what really should be a non-problematic operation, I got a very different view of the problem. I found that in the same way that office work is not identical to procedural specifications, instructions never really unambiguously and completely tell you what to do. Everyone who remembers their first attempt at following a recipe, or trying to assemble some kind of do-it-yourself gadget, knows that this is the case. The reasons that it is the case have to do with the basic indeterminancy of the ways that we talk about the world.

That indeterminacy means that to follow instructions really is a substantial task, and that the interface to a machine like a copier is never entirely constructed by the designer. What the designer provides are collections of clues, and particularly in the case of a self-explanatory interface, the user's task then is to take those clues and reconstruct them into what the designer intended him or her to do with the machine. The designer relies on the user to make that discovery, and the user relies on the designer to make the use of the machine discoverable.

These two studies showed me that the tasks of carrying out procedures and following instructions are essentially problematic. My own hunch is that they are problematic by nature, not by accident, and that they will always be so. The work that is required for these projects isn't due to the inadequacy of instructions. While bad instructions may add to that work, good instructions will never eliminate it. The trouble that people encounter doing these tasks, the work that's required, is just in the nature of the beast. The success that people have at doing these tasks relies on some very fundamental skills, which, because they are so fundmental and so frequently applied, are almost entirely taken for granted.

This then is my concern: that the kinds of folk theories that identify work with procedures or instructions will miss the actual work that's involved. The actual work is the business of applying general descriptions to actual events in all of their real worldly detail. Now it's not clear what an adequate understanding of that ability would mean with respect to the design of technology. It does seem clear, however, that current interface designs, by simply embodying folk theories of these activities, continue to ignore much of the work that actually goes on in the office, or in learning to operate an unfamiliar machine. As a consequence, that work remains outside the bounds of both the theory and the technology that's built upon it.

The advent of computer-based technologies presents the opportunity to use and abuse other common-sense theories of human behavior, particularly theories about social interaction. I won't go into what I see as the troubles of the "human-machine interaction" metaphor here, however. Instead I want in closing to recommend an alternative for design: briefly, that we make the relationship between common-sense folk theories about the world and actual practices the subject for research.

Now, to give you a sense of what that might yield, I want to talk for a minute about some of the more recent applications of what is called Cognitive Science, and some of the developing capabilities of interactive computer-based systems. I think these prototypes demonstrate the possibility that rather than designing systems that attempt to preclude trouble, systems could be designed that would actually support the negotiation of trouble in doing work. I'll describe very briefly a prototype system that was designed within the group that I work with at Xerox PARC called the Cognitive and Instructional Sciences group. The system is called RABBIT and it's designed for situations where a user is trying to make use of a data base, but where she doesn't quite know what's there in the data base, or how to get at it. A query of a data base is an attempt to describe what you are after, but you often don't know what the terms of that description should be.

RABBIT uses restaurants as a very simple example. So we have a data base of restaurants, and the user asks the data base to tell her about Chinese restaurants in Palo Alto. What RABBIT will do is come back with an example of a Chinese restaurant in Palo Alto that is open from 11:00 in the morning to 11:00 at night, and accepts Mastercharge. Now from the example the user sees that the system knows about two other attributes of restaurants, that is, what their hours are and whether they accept credit cards. The user can then pick any of those attributes and reformulate the initial query. So she can go back and say, well, I'm looking for Chinese restaurants in Palo Alto that are open at

8:00 in the morning. And together, essentially, the user and the system can construct the right query, going back and forth between this general description and these examples, which show what the terms of the general description can, in fact, be.

What RABBIT does, in other words, is to support the process of repairing or reformulating an initial query until it's right, rather than demanding that the user know the terms of the query before sitting down to make it. RABBIT does that by recognizing something of how a query actually gets constructed, and taking advantage of some of the ways that people actually use the technology.

The implications of all this for research are that we need to begin to not just rely on our common sense, but to make common sense itself a topic for study. One place to start is by coming to understand the relation of folk theories of human behavior to the actual situation and events they describe. In studying that relation we must neither confuse common sense accounts with actual practices, nor dismiss them as just stories. The relation of common sense accounts to actual practices is indefinitely more interesting than a question of truth or falsity, correctness or inaccuracy. Only if that relationship is understood will the theories rest on solid ground and be useful to the design of technology. The ultimate users of the technology, whose work it claims to support, should demand nothing less.

Staff Participation in Office Systems' Design:
Two Case Studies at the World Bank

Richard E. Barry
Administrative Operations Coordinator
World Bank

Let me begin by saying that I am here not here in my capacity as an official of the World Bank, but more in the capacity of a person who has led three major systems design efforts at the World Bank that involved a lot of worker participation. I have led some others as well. One was the design of an information word processing system that had not yet been installed in the Eastern Africa region of the bank. The offices are in Washington, and the project affected about 300 staff, about one-third of them secretarial. The second case study, one I'm presently engaged in, concerns the design of building facilities for the whole bank, so it affects about 6,000 people. The third one, which has to do with designing a long-range strategic planning model, we will not have time to go into. So we'll be talking about the first two cases.

I approach this topic with some humility because I know about all the good work going on in Canada, Europe and Scandinavia. Perhaps we can shed some light on the processes of designing systems for contemporary workplaces. Also, it's always dangerous when you present an upbeat case, because people go away thinking that everything is sweetness and light when it's not. We have had plenty of problems to face in the World Bank, and we have tackled some of them and have a long way to go with others.

If there is one thing we should be getting out of this conference, it is the need for a vision of the future, a vision that focuses on making effective use of people. We have been too busy plugging things into walls and making them work. We need to look at the dimensions of work. There has been too much focusing on the dimensions of black boxes. We need to focus on dimensions such as work diversification, work enrichment and productivity. We need to develop a vision that has a large place for human relationships and for consideration of things like privacy. I think some of the systems that we are now developing will have some of these dimensions much more than in the past.

And we need to shape that vision in the workplace, by listening to the people who use these systems. And to do that you need to involve the staff. Common sense, it's still the best of all the scientific methods, I think. We need to involve staff at the earliest stages of the process. And that's what I will talk about using these case studies.

Following are two charts that depict the two studies I mentioned. They are particularly interesting in their differences. One was very

CASE 1:

The Washington, D.C. Offices of the Eastern Africa Region (1978)

- Purpose was to determine a strategy for WP support.

- A user without a system looking for one.

- Bound by bank-wide policies/plans under the responsibility of central support departments (personnel, administration, office technology).

- Very limited technical resources in field of office technology systems. Technical support for the Central Support Departments.

CASE II:

The Washington, D.C. Offices of The Administrative Services (1982)

- Purpose was to establish the impact of office technology on facilities: macro-building criteria and micro work stations.

- A supplier of office support services and systems (space, furniture, power, HVAC, etc.). Planning facilities "futures."

- Planning for buildings with multiple users, multiple systems.

- Master of bank-wide facilities policies/plan.

- Very limited technical resources in field of office technology systems. Technical support from user departments.

- The decision to involve staff: doing it for the right reasons; management involvement and communication; getting meaningful involvement.

- Terms of reference (TOR) for the design/planning study: productivity and job satisfaction; task force acceptance/modification of TOR; focus on organization/work issues; priority of TF work—letting everyone know; consulting support to TF—technical/process.

- Providing interim support.

much a group of unsophisticated users, without a grounding in technology, deciding what they wanted to do with office automation in an institution with a highly centralized word processing environment. The other, where we are talking about the design of whole buildings, we have a bunch of building people and administrative people, of whom I am one, who had very little technical resources in terms of information systems.

The main thing is the decision to involve the staff, and doing it for the right reasons. The literature is full of the participative approach to management as a way to let people blow off steam, to make them feel good, and as a generally healthy thing to do. But participation in this way plays it safe. All of those things may be true, but there are some interesting other reasons to do it. Basically, it's a way of getting some better decisions.

We used a number of methods, the principal one among them the use of a task force composed of individuals from across the spectrum of the organization; not just the secretaries group, but from all over the organization. We did it by organization, functional responsibility, level of staff and other dimensions as well. At first we tried to cover everything and, of course, discovered that we had a committee that was much too large. So we started combining the dimensions and got about a dozen people, about half support staff and half the so-called professional staff.

In the second case it was reverse situation. (We have about 10 owned and 10 leased buildings in a multi-block area in downtown Washington, so there were a lot of physical problems.) So in the second case we got representation from all the major users, who were very systems-oriented people and knew their systems and knew what the future of those systems would be.

The potential benefits of the participative approach include: more committment from staff, a greater sense of involvement, the build up of new informal communication patterns, and the build up of the problem-solving capacity of individuals and the organization as a whole. But most important, you get better decisions. That's the thing to sell management on, better decisions, and this does employ the common sense approach.

There are problems, though, with significant staff involvement. It takes a lot longer up front. Hopefully it will take less time downstream, because if you do a better job in the design you have fewer implementation problems.

The process also breaks down communication barriers, and it's difficult to do that. If you haven't asked somebody for their opinion for 10 years, it's difficult to get them to come out and express their feelings. This is one of the problems we had engaging the secretarial staff. It takes a lot of training as you go along, and issues get raised which are not directly germaine. You are creating problems that you never had before.

It also creates a lot of stress by taking people away from their regular work. The legitimacy of their role in this process has to be established, and the secretaries often are their own worst enemies is this respect. Supervisory secretaries were often much less forgiving when the phones were ringing and things had to be done, than were the principals to whom the secretaries were responsible.

It raises a lot of expectations, and you better be sure you can deliver, or else you are going to have a lot more problems. And once you start it, there is no going back. So, that can be a problem.

And most importantly, it may not turn out the way you want it to. Once the floor is open and you try to get concensus, you may find that you are the one that's not concensusing. So you'd better be prepared for that. Also, I may focus too much on job satisfaction. We set two objectives: group productivity and group job satisfaction. There had to be something in it for everybody. But the tendency was to focus too much on job satisfaction, while there is an urgent need for improved productivity in the office. We have to tackle this problem as well in a humane and sensible manner. If you never look at the productivity angle, you'll never get managers, at least after the first time, to agree to this kind of approach.

Let me just run through some of the contributions that were made by different people. This is very interesting, because it is very specific as to what things certain people on those task forces really contributed. The secretaries couldn't wait to get their hands on the machines, and it was very difficult to get them to focus on conceptual problems at first. They had seen some demonstrations and were undergoing some training because they knew nothing about office technology. It helped to have higher level staff there to say: wait, there's a lot of hardware that can do a lot of things, but what we have got to look at is the organization, whether to centralize or decentralize things, who is going to control it, and who is going to be responsible.

We used central support department staff, personnel staff, and organizational development staff to give us technical support, to help us through some of the planning assumptions that were external to the region. And we used process consultants, of which Leslie Schneider was one. Process consultants were most effective in helping to keep things on track; finding out about the hidden agenda items that were really bugging people and tracing them down in between meetings. They got people together, resolved some personal issues, and helped in teaching the participants how to participate. So you've got professional staff who know very much how to contribute to meetings. Suddenly you have secretaries, and you want them to chair some of the meetings, and they don't have the skills, so you have to train them. If they are not always articulate or well versed in writing, or speaking, you've got to bring that out. And the process consultants can help.

The impacts we looked at, principally, were the working relationships and the office spaces. We looked at alternative organizations from the highest, most centralized, to the lowest, least centralized. That's what we selected, not the inbetween. Why? Because it would destroy the team effort. Secretaries were saying things like: "Hey, if I'm out working on this appraisal report on the loan to the Sudan, I don't know what your priorities are as things stand now. I don't know when I answer the phone who is working on what report and whether I should let them through. If we are working on this thing together, I know what your priorities are. I know what phone calls to put off or let through."

That's the kind of design criteria that came from the secretaries. We surveyed the things they like the least, and wanted to design out things like repetitive typing while increasing the capability to handle bilingual material and more difficult numerical tables. The higher-level staff wanted better turn-around time, better linking with data processing, and improved controls over work. So each group got some action, and they better understood where the other one was coming from.

The health factors we looked at included office space and rest breaks. In this study we proposed an opthamological monitoring program—a recommendation of the secretaries—and it was instituted as a result. We also looked at a systematic training program and getting more information out about the design criteria for the hardware that one would ultimately use.

The principal conclusion of the first case, the Eastern Africa Region offices, was that there was a strong preference for a fully decentralized approach for several reasons: (1) a concern with improving and intensifying working relationships; and (2) a far-reaching concern with maintaining and strengthening divisional responsibility for, and control over, its own work and its capacity to plan its work, as well as to ensure proper quality control.

The second case is ongoing. The principal conclusion here, looking at building construction, was that there was an exponential decrease in the ratio of people to terminals foreseen in the future. Indeed, the major impacts of office technology on present and future systems relate to landscaping, power supply, HVAC, lighting and furnishings.

In conclusion, let me show you what we were able to do by talking to all of these users throughout the bank. From 1977 to 1980, the ratio of people to terminals was reduced by a factor of four. Between 1980 and 1983, it dropped by a factor of six. We're predicting that it will go to one to one, depending on which scenario you believe, somewhere between 1985 and 1988. And it will probably exceed one to one.

The telephone is a good analogy, a good harbinger in an information rich organization like the World Bank. We have a ratio of 1.2 telephones per staff member. If it is an information tool we are happy to use it. So we are going to have 5 buildings that accomodate this. A terminal puts out about the same number of BTUs as a person. So if you're building a building for 1,200 people, as we just did, you are going to have to have ventilation for 2,400 people, according to the one to one scenario. These are the things we have to look at.

Strengthening Group Solidarity of Clericals: A Case Study

Janine Morgall
Department of Sociology
Lund University, Sweden

This is a story of a secretary group consisting of 10 women working at a small research institute at the University of Copenhagen. I was a member of this group and union shop steward during the period of time when word processing equipment was introduced in this institute.

The unusual thing about this particular group is that due to several historical factors at the institute, the group worked independently and had very little supervision by the academic staff. Because of this the secretaries had close to 100% control over the decision making and introduction of word processing equipment into their workplace. For years the secretaries had been meeting every month to plan and coordinate their work and it was at these meetings that the discussions and decisions about word processing took place.

In this presentation I would like to cover two things:

FIRST   to give a brief history of this process, emphasizing the problems encountered by the group, and

SECOND   to give a list of activities which resulted from the group's experiences and increased consciousness.

In 1979, funds became available at the institute for the purpose of purchasing office and computer equipment. The secretary group decided to investigate the possibilities of word processing equipment. At this time very little had been written about new office technology in the Danish press and the group was ignorant of the discussions on occupational health hazards and organizational problems which were then going on in England, the U.S. and other parts of Scandinavia. They therefore only saw the word processor as an "advanced typewriter" which would be a help to them in their heavy typing load.

They began their study of word processing equipment by arranging for the entire group to visit and talk with a group of word processing operators at a local publishing company in Copenhagen. Next the group visited a showroom for word processing equipment and had the salesperson demonstrate the equipment. The group then informed the academic staff that they intended to use some of the funds for word processing equipment. In the democratic tradition of the institute a word processing committee was set up. It consisted of three secretaries (among them the shop steward), and one programmer and one member of the academic staff (both male).

The task of this group was to evaluate and select the system best suited to the needs of the institute and to make a recommendation to the institute board as to what system to buy.

In the meantime the secretary group was slowly becoming aware of some of the problems associated with word processing equipment, which they discussed not only at their monthly meetings but also at meetings called to specifically to discuss these issues. Initially they were not very worried because they felt they had the situation in hand. They did , however, draw up a checklist to be used by the three secretaries who sat on the word processing committee. The checklist included a list of functions and features they wanted in a machine, as well as things to watch out for which could be potential occupational health hazards.

When the secretaries, checklist in hand, began firing questions at the salesmen, it became apparent that the salesmen were not accustomed to dealing with such well-prepared customers who knew exectly what they wanted. Much to the anger of the secretaries, their questions were often ignored or in many cases not taken seriously. One example of this: when a secretary made a remark about the screaming green letters on a screen, she was told by the salesman that all you had to do was pull a pair of pantyhose over the screen to avoid eyestrain.

Another example: one salesman used two different sales pitches— one for the secretaries and one for the academic staff. He told the secretaries how the equipment would save them time and help them in their work; then he later took the academics aside and told them how many secretary positions they could save by buying this system.

Because of the way the secretaries were treated, combined with the increasing contact with written materials from outside Denmark, the group became increasingly mistrustful of the salesmen and their products. They also became unsure about whether or not they could in fact handle the potential problems, especially the VDTs. At last they decided to start slowly and make an initial investment in a small word processing machine WITHOUT a screen.

Training was the next problem after the purchase. The group feared that if only one or two secretaries were trained on the machine, they would inadvertently be creating their own typing pool. They therefore made one of the conditions of the sale the possibility for all 10 secretaries to be trained on the machine—free of charge. This was done by playing one salesman off against the other.

There were several problems with the training. First of all the course was so poorly organized that there were no written instructions available at the training sessions. All instruction came from an instructor who kept disappearing. Secondly, they did not give a conceptual overview of the system but only instructions in manual functions. Thirdly, it took more than five months before they got the manual translated into the Danish language.

Next the group faced the problem of introducing the word processor into the workplace. The biggest difficulty was combating the unrealistic expectations the academic staff had about the equipment. They began pressuring the secretaries, showing little understanding when they explained how little they had learned on the course and how they needed to practice before they could become proficient in using the machine effectively. They also began telling the secretaries WHAT should be typed on the machines — based not on knowledge of the machine but on the myth that technology makes everything go faster and more efficiently.

After an introduction period and a lot of discussion the secretaries decided to apply for three more word processors, also without screens.

This entire process resulted in an awareness and increased solidarity within the group which resulted in many activities.

- Together the group held a meeting for other members of the clerical workers union where they shared their experiences in the decision-making, selecting, buying and introducing of word processors into the office.
- They were interviewed in the university newspaper which resulted in many secretaries calling and asking advice on selecting word processing equipment.
- They wrote up their experiences and assembled it into a short photocopied report. This report became very popular in Denmark and was used by secretaries and researchers alike.
- Members of the group have been asked to give talks both within and outside the union.
- The group wrote an article about their experiences which is appearing in a special issue of the magazine of the Danish women's movement on office technology.
- One of the secretaries is now sitting on the technology committee of the University of Copenhagen.
- Several secretaries are either taking courses or participating in workshops on new office technology.

In such a brief presentation it is very difficult to describe the experiences and the processes which this group of secretaries had over a period of many years. These experiences changed the group and the individuals involved forever, and resulted in a strengthened group solidarity. The point of this short case study is to emphasize the importance of the need for office workers to work together, discuss together and document their experiences so that they can be shared with other clerical workers. Research by professional researchers is important but not as important nor as effective at eliciting change as increased awareness, involvement and activities of the clerical workers themselves.

The Decline of the "Secretary as Generalist"

Mary Murphree
Center for the Study of Women & Society
City University of New York

A secretary for many years on Wall Street, and then in academia, before finding my way into graduate school, I am an industrial sociologist, or more precisely an office sociologist. What I hope to do today is put a little historical flesh on the office automation process as secretaries in the U.S. have experienced it. I will also talk about how managers and personnel administrators see the secretarial job changing with the introduction of word processing. How do they define the situation, both as individuals and as groups? And how—with vendors and consultants—are they dealing with it?

I will mainly be talking about megafirms, Wall Street law firms, in particular the largest pacesetting firms. I collected my data there and will draw on a case study I did of a single huge firm, and from interviews I conducted with managers and attorneys across a large number of firms.

Office automation is a term referring to a process of change. Sociologists often use the term "rationalization" for that process. It is a concept developed by Max Weber which means the subdivision (specialization) and mechanization of work in its many forms. For the secretarial occupation in America it is a long-term process in which the occupation has been hit over the years by a series of new technologies and has had its tasks taken away and assigned to other workers.

The prevailing stereotype traditionally, however, of the secretarial occupation has been one of "the private secretary"—the secretary working for one man. A good way to look at this is in terms of the job this person was doing, so I call this the secretary as generalist, or "Jill of all Trades."

As a generalist, the private secretary was doing much or all of the support services—the typing, filing, copying—that we will see later have been divided up between a number of departments. She was also doing a fair number of quasi-professional tasks: some lawyering in the law firm (doing research, collecting library data), some administration (accounting, and doing certain personnel functions). She was also doing her share of domestic work, cleaning and cooking, if you will.

What were the authority or control relations that defined her job? She was also an "office wife," and we owe a great debt of gratitude to Rosabeth Kanter for spelling out the patrimonial, feudal relationship that existed between the boss and secretary—based on loyalty, arbitrary power of the boss, mobility tied to that boss, the source of all rewards and punishments. Nonetheless, the traditional secretary had a fair amount of variety, autonomy and responsibility in her job—things, I will argue, which have been taken away from her at a greater cost than many of us have realized.

In 1977, when I began to analyze what was going on with legal secretaries, the secretary as skilled generalist was very much the prevailing stereotype. It was also increasingly a myth, seriously out of sync with what more and more people were experiencing. The vocational education schools were still teaching women to prepare themselves to go into the office and "hitch their wagon" to the star that Helen Gurley Brown promised in the late 1960s. That is, use your bean, play your cards right, hook up with a man who is going somewhere, and you, too, can make it to the top and into the executive suite. But this traditional model—with its benefits (and costs)—was on its way out, to be replaced by a more rigid, impersonal, rationalized office.

It is particularly observable in the big law firms today. These giant factories are the quintessential examples of a specialized and mechanized world where secretarial work is subdivided among dozens of automated service departments and para-professionals (paralegals, legal librarians, proofreaders, etc.)

The last gasp in this rationalization process, of course, has come with the introduction of specialized word processing departments. At their centralized worst (word processing centers), they represent the point when the quintessential secretarial task, typing, also gets taken away from the secretary and turned over to a department some four floors away.

Authority relations among secretaries and bosses are changing as well. As C. Wright Mills and Harry Braverman warned in their works, the old social office is breaking down. Today there are centralized personnel administrators replacing the boss as the source of reward and punishment. You have more controls and more impersonal, rigid rules, formal year-end reviews by the personnel department, docking for tardiness, dress codes, etc. Secretaries must "please" Personnel as well as their individual attorneys. This is producing a state of supervisory ambiguity. Who do I work for? secretaries ask. Who is going to reward me? Who carries the most weight, my boss or Personnel? How should I handle this period of transition?

I should point out here parenthetically that these personnel departments are undergoing their own revolution as a new cadre of trained experts come in. Personnel used to be a good upward route for career-oriented secretaries, but the old-timers (women) are falling by the wayside as "numbers men" from the corporate world take over the top administrative jobs.

Ask management why these changes and they will tell you about "the secretarial shortage," and how they have to hire women with low skills. They also grumble about women's rising expectations and the problems the women's movement has created. "Look who we are getting," they say, "no one wants to be a secretary any more." Turnover is high. Morale is low. One thing corporate executives want more than anything—lawyers especially hate problems they can't solve—is a happy office. They want an office that they can feel good about themselves in. On the bright side, by the way, there is a very interesting collusion of corporate wives with secretaries. Many wives, typically, are telling their husbands they can't give the family checkbook to the secretary; that they shouldn't refer to her as their "girl," etc. Managers also will complain, of course, about the cost of clerical overhead—while professional salaries skyrocket.

Hence the interest in word processing. Vendors are naturally eagerly exploiting managements' unhappiness and making some rather fabulous promises. Word processing is not only cheaper, and will reduce your labor costs, but it's more efficient ("faster turn-around time") and the quality of your production will go up, they claim. Furthermore, you can turn the turnover problem into a plus by hiring part-time people, training them quickly, and not paying them benefits. In sum, you can get around the women's movement and the morale problems it creates—these machines don't "talk back." And you can avoid the secretarial shortage. Companies also want word processing because the guy down the street has it. There is a study from New Jersey that documents this. "Keeping up with Jones & Jones" enters into the decision, even if it doesn't necessarily enhance productivity.

However, most companies quickly learn that automating isn't as easy as it sounds. So the next thing they do is hire consultants. The consultants come in with all sorts of solutions. Create an aura of participation, they say. Get yourself a clerical committee of secretaries. Be straight when you hire people and tell them they will have to work for two or three people and hire only those who agree. Use attrition to dump the "bad apples"—let them go somewhere else and don't replace them.

Another recommendation typically made by consultants has been to centralize the repetitive jobs in a word processing center—though farsighted consultants have always judiciously resisted this—and decentralize the non-routine jobs at word processing satellite stations. Tuck these centers away in the core of your skyscrapers. Simplify the procedures and hire minorities and older women returning to the labor force for these jobs. They'll work for far less and expect less. This can get around the skill shortage and save money too. (Anne Machung is going to tell us in greater detail what it feels like to work in these shops.) Paraprofessionalize your other clerical jobs. Save the women on your staffs who want career mobility for your decentralized "satellite" word processing machines. Use your smarter secretaries here—you'll have to pay them more of course—and give them new names (such as, in the law, "legal programmer" or "legal technician"). Let them handle the idiosyncratic tasks, the time emergencies, the lower level research tasks private secretaries formerly handled. It will solve the "women's libber" problem and let you tap a higher skill level to boot.

At consulting conferences this process is summarized in the phrase: "Move $10,000 work off of $30,000 desks." For law firms this merely means stop paying junior lawyers $45,000 to do work a woman with a B.A. degree will do for $18,000, or if you're lucky, $12,000. The idea is to hire bright, seven-sister graduates to work in close proximity with the attorneys. They'll speak the same language as the legal staff; the lawyers will be more comfortable; and firms can bill clients for their time.

Essentially, of course, such advice merely perpetuates—and even exacerbates—the caste-like properties of our large organizations. When followed it encourages a kind of "technological discrimination," creating a few good (upgraded, higher paid) word processing jobs at the satellites, and many more deskilled, lower paid, sweatshop-type jobs in the centers.

Turning Secretaries into Word Processors:
Some Fiction and a Fact or Two

Anne Machung
Institute for the Study of Social Change
University of California, Berkeley

Over the past four years I have interviewed secretaries and word processors in large banks, insurance companies and law firms in San Francisco for work connected with my dissertation. Since all word processing equipment was centralized at that time (1978-81), all of the operators I interviewed were working in large centers. Today, I want to present some of the conclusions I have reached from that work, comparing what my respondents told me to what the trade journal and management literature has to say about word processing. Needless to say, these are quite at variance with each other.

First, to talk a bit about the trade journal literature. Over and over again, in a thousand different ways, trade journals claim that large corporations today are automating their offices in order to increase clerical productivity and reduce labor costs. Since drafts and letters can be printed out faster on word processing equipment than at a conventional typewriter, fewer secretaries are needed. Hence they see the reduction in labor costs coming about mainly through attrition in the secretarial ranks. Basically, corporations want to substitute word processing machines for secretaries. And because secretaries will leave by attrition, they see this "reduction in labor costs" as a somewhat benign process.

Today, I would like to counter these claims and suggest otherwise: that by automating the office, large corporations are neither lowering clerical labor costs nor increasing clerical productivity. Rather, by substituting word processing machines for typewriters, and word processing operators for secretaries, they are raising costs of production, increasing discontent in the clerical ranks, and undermining jobs and job skills historically valued by women—all under the guise of "technical progress."

There is, for one, little systematic evidence that word processing increases clerical productivity. Much of the secretarial job, for example, does not involve typing but rather social, organizational, and diplomatic work (connecting people to people), and this cannot easily be automated. A 1981 article in **ComputerWorld** by Steven Abraham reported, too, that typing accounts for only about 1.2% of all white collar productivity. So even if corporations were able to increase the productivity of each secretary with word processing equipment, they could hardly increase white collar productivity to any great extent.

Secondly, there is little systematic evidence either that word processing reduces clerical labor costs. There were nearly 4 million secretaries in the U.S. in 1970 and nearly 5 million in 1980. If anything, secretaries, as the Department of Labor reports, are one of the fastest growing occupational sectors in the U.S. today, despite the massive introduction of word processing equipment into U.S. business offices in the 1970s and 1980s. Office automation has not reduced their aggregate numbers at all. Moreover, clerical salaries account for approximately one-quarter of all white collar overhead costs; three-quarters of that money goes to pay managerial salaries. Reducing the number of secretaries, even if it could be done, would not really reduce white collar labor costs very much. It is managers who are expensive, not secretaries.

Lastly, corporations talk a lot about "cost-justifying" word processing, but only, as Driscoll (1981) has noted, before the fact; seldom are attempts made to cost-justify word processing after it has been installed. Once installed, the equipment is assumed to be cost-effective, but this assumption is never tested. Why this lag in determining if the equipment has indeed lived up to its promises—if indeed it has not? So what, then, in going on? After personally interviewing secretaries and word processors about their jobs, it seems to me that the kinds of personal and patriarchal controls that historically have characterized secretarial-managerial relationships are breaking down. Across the country, secretaries want better paid jobs, more respect, and a chance at promotions—just like managers. But corporations are loath to give them that and discontent in the secretarial ranks is deepening. Despite such discontent, corporations continue to need (or want) a docile, submissive, relatively literate group of women to work for low wages. The bifurcation between what clerical workers want and what business is willing to offer is growing, and business sees automation as one way out of that dilemma. Automation, they claim throughout the business and trade journal literature, "upgrades" clerical skills, creates new career paths, and transforms dull, routine and repetitious jobs into something challenging and creative. It answers, that is, clerical complaints about their jobs.

But does it really? Let's take the question of skills, for example. Vendors sell word processing equipment to corporations, telling them it takes only a day or so at most to train a new operator. But what kind of skill takes so little time to learn? What skills indeed? Operators themselves are not fooled. As one word processor working at a San Francisco insurance company told me:

> When I first started out, I did take a little bit more pride in the fact that these letters don't look too bad, or whatever. Well, they can't look too bad! After a while you realize that even the most ridiculously lousy typist and beginner could still come up with a perfect letter, but at first it's like magic; it looks good.

As Mary Murphree has pointed out, secretarial work historically has consisted of a complex array of skills: diplomacy, tact, finesse, and organizational know-how. Typing was just one part of the secretarial job, and the most boring part. But as secretaries are turned into word processing operators, such social and organizational skills are eliminated from their jobs. Typing becomes the only skill that is needed. "You don't need much," as one word processing operator reminded me, "to talk to a machine."

New "machine skills," then, are replacing "out-moded" social and organizational skills. But what, besides typing, is meant by these new machine skills? One operator, herself blind, told me it took her three months to really master her machine. But after that she became extremely bored because the work was so routine. Her story is hardly unique, but is repeated time and time again by sighted word processing operators. One supervisor, in fact, told me she had to replace operators after two or three years because they "burn out." Using their minds too little, their eyes too much, and doing the same thing over and over each day fatigues them enormously. And as they burn out, their productivity drops precipitously—not because the machine can't do the work, but because no person can perform so repetitiously for so long a period. The new "machine skill," then consists, in part, of the "ability" to sit in front of a terminal, doing work which increasingly becomes repetitious and monotonous, for hours at a time, or months, without becoming bored, and without "burning out." Yet word processing is one basis for telling clerical women that office automation upgrades their skills, their career paths, and their mobility. I call this "double-talk," and I think this is happening not to increase mobility between the secretarial and managerial labor force, but to eliminate it.

As one discontented secretary said to me, following a particularly unhappy job experience:

> Up until then, I always thought, "Well, men go into executive positions just kind of like by miracle or something. They're smart; they get into these positions." And here I realized that I was doing a lot of his job. For one thing, he wasn't interested in the job anymore, so he kept trying to pass off more and more to me. When I left there, I was about a year and a half with him, I thought: "I am just as bright as he, so why am I doing this at $15,000 less than what he is doing? Why am I being a secretary?"

It is, in part, because of challenges like this that large corporations are shifting to word processing, isolating discontented secretaries into word processing centers, and eliminating skills on the job. Very shortly, many large corporations fear they will have to start recognizing secretarial skills and paying secretaries what they are really worth. And that may mean paying top secretaries $30,000 a year or more. But one way to eliminate claims for equal pay and equality of opportunity is to eliminate the basis for making these claims. Word processing operators lack the social and organizational skills secretaries traditionally have acquired on their jobs and lack the experience that would teach them that. Transforming secretaries into word processing operators therefore eliminates skills from the job. And it also eliminates the right to claim mobility and higher salaries based upon growing skills and experience. Word processing, as such, entrenches women deeper into the clerical ghetto.

By automating the office, therefore, large corporations are not so much increasing clerical productivity and reducing labor costs, as they are reducing skills in the secretarial job and creating an even more low paid, highly expendible, and interchangeable labor force. Only these are now called word processing operators, not secretaries. And what they do is considered technical work, not personal work. Is this progress?

IV. Occupational Health and the Computerized Office

Office Computerization:
Research Then and Now
Olov Östberg
Central Organization of
Salaried Employees, Sweden

Office computerization continues, and so does the discussion of its effects. The title of the present paper draws from my review "Office Computerization in Sweden", which was presented at an international symposium in 1976. The subtitle of the paper contained the following keywords:

- Worker participation
- Workplace design
- Visual strain

Five years later, when the paper was eventually published in a symposium proceedings, the editor declared that the proceedings had in no way become outdated and that the subject area had in fact become more vital over the years. Speaking of my own paper, I agree that the subtitle covers areas that are no less hot today than in 1976. During the past six years, however, there has been a broadening of the scene and a displacement of the center of gravity of the discussion. An equivalent paper written today would also have to cover these keywords:

- Standards and regulations
- Structural changes
- National R & D projects

The following discourse will deal with the above six areas, but will also encompass a comparison between Sweden/Scandinavia/Europe and the USA.

Once Upon a Time...

It is supposed to be the privilege of old wise men to sit down and reflect over past times. At the age of 42 I am not old, chronologically speaking, and the present paper will perhaps indicate that I am not even wise. I shall nevertheless throughout this paper provide some personal reflections on the short history of office computerization.

My professional contact with office computerization dates back to 1970, when I was hired to work as an ergonomist with the Swedish Co-op. This organization was actually, and still is, one of the largest private employers in Sweden. Its reputation for being a progressive organization showed up, among other things, in its early recognition of the need for ergonomics in the area of office computerization. The head of the Co-op's ergonomics lab was Toni Ivergard, whose interest in this area, in 1972, was manifested in a doctoral dissertation on the ergonomics of new technology and the information thru-putting of check-out cashiers.

I was involved in the selection of Video Display Terminals (VDTs) and the design of VDT work stations for the data system dealing with inventories and purchase orders sent from the Co-op sales-points to the Co-op warehouses. The work has been documented in a M.Sc. project report by Colin Mackay (1971). Dr. Mackay is today responsible for issuing British health and safety criteria documents in connection with the employment of new technology.

The evaluation of VDTs resulted in a ranking list among those VDTs which met the technical criteria set by the Co-op's computer mainframes. Olivetti and Facit were deemed to have the most ergonomiclly sound terminals, whereas for example Alfascope got a less favorable ranking. The same type of ergonomics ranking has recently been published by Professor Grandjean's research group in Switzerland (Fellman et al., 1982). It is not a sheer coincidence that the Swedish Aflascope terminal obtained the best marks this time. Rather, it is the result of the manufacturer's determination to make use of the criticism of the early 70's (see also Hultgren & Knave, 1974).

The Co-op's data system was too constraining to allow a decent design of the VDT work stations and work tasks, and at that time there was also no VDT office furniture on the market. The VDTs were to be used in a back-up function to a system designed around an Optical Character Reading (OCR) machine. Forms had to be filled in at the sales-points round the country, and the task of quite a few of the headquarter VDT operators was simply to key in the numbers that the OCR machine had not been able to recognize. All forms with one or more discarded numbers were put in a pile, and without changing the queue-order, the VDT operators had to reach one-by-one for a form, look at the screen to see which numbers were unidentified, key in the correct numbers, reach for another form, etc.

The OCR machine was a marvel, had it not been for the fact that people at the sales-points insisted on writing the number 7 the Swedish way (with a cross-bar and a wavy top), to make the number 0 too thin and not make the ends meet, to put the number slightly outside the number boxes, etc. The resulting VDT jobs were bound to be paced, monotonous, repetitive, degrading, and straining to both body and mind. Under such conditions, office computerization becomes a source of misery rather than a helpful tool, and the VDT becomes the scapegoat.

Ergonomics: The Pudding is the Proof

Today's puddings are baked in a highly competitive international market. To the consumers, and hence to the producers, the very pudding is the proof whether it is good or not.

Despite the resistance of many manufacturers and employer representatives, the forces of the market have brought about quite a dramatic change in the design and utilization of VDTs. It has become commonplace for manufacturers and vendors to claim that the latest VDT is ergonomically improved and designed to prevent postural and visual fatigue. Yet these marketing people had earlier maintained that the often heard complaints from VDT operators could be traced to the operators rather than to the VDT *per se*. During a study tour in the US in 1981, I often heard comments from influential VDT manufacturers the essence of which was:

> Sweden represents one per cent of our market, but due to your leading role in work environment issues we pay three per cent attention to your arguments. We believe that your emphasis on ergonomics in the form of detachable keyboards, tiltable screens, etc., only marginally helps improving office productivity. However, our sales statistics for Sweden and other European countries shows that this lack of link between ergonomics and productivity seems not to bother you. So then we too have to compete with ergonomic design features.

If the end-users of computer systems, i.e., the VDT operators, have a say in the purchasing of new computer equipment, it is obvious that manufacturers and vendors have little to gain in belittling operator complaints. In this respect, 'the pudding is the proof' of ergonomics.

And in this respect the USA is now going through the process that took place in Europe some five years ago.

Certainly there are differences. The European tradition is that unions, employer federations, and governmental bodies, have workable contacts (relatively speaking) between them, and that somehow a mutual understanding/acceptance becomes visible in the melting pot. Industrial relations agreements, product standards, and national safety and health regulations, are then formed in a positive atmosphere (again relatively speaking) in order that the introduction of new technology shall not be put to a stop at the local bargaining table.

That this formula works for Sweden is perhaps shown by the fact that Sweden, with regard to the size of the population, has a larger share of VDTs, industrial robots, numerically controlled machine tools, etc., than any other country in the world. With the prospect of being granted a real influence on the computerization process, Swedish unions typically welcome new technology because it "will then be regarded as a support technology and subservient to social decisions in society" (Boivie & Ostberg, 1982).

In the US, the concept of freedom of the market seems to have been stretched also to mean freedom from standards and regulations (and unions). What is considered to 'pave the way' in Europe, becomes 'interfering roadblocks' in the US.

It is true that premature standards and regulations in theory might be a hindrance in the development, and thus might act as interfering roadblocks on the way towards positive solutions. In reality it is more likely that unfounded or obsolete standards and regulations will be changed or simply neglected in the course of the technical development. One such case would be the Swedish safety and health regulation concerning VDTs (Swedish NBOSH, 1978), which *overlooked* the possibility that VDTs with black characters on white background might become flicker free and superior to traditional VDTs with luminous characters on a dark background. As a matter of fact, Sweden recently *proposed* an ergonomic ISO standard for VDTs, the foundation of which is that black characters on white background is the best solution for office applications of VDTs (Swedish CIS, 1982). To this can be argued that in five years time we will have liquid crystal VDTs that ergonomically are superior to today's VDTs based on cathode ray tube (CRT) technique. The long perspective, however, must not be a crippling handicap in attempts to solve the problems in a shorter term perspective.

What Seems to be the Problem of VDT Workplaces?

Ergonomists dealing with *person-computer interaction* in production systems will sooner or later find themselves in the territory of *worker-management interactions*. Office systems management, and the computer industry, are reluctant to accept the findings of problem surveys and field studies drawing on VDT operators' own statements. An ergonomist dependent on traditional research funding will in those circumstances find it troublesome to exhibit attitudes like "It looks like there are workplace problems linked to the use of VDTs, so let's be sensitive and try to delineate the problem areas", and will more likely put it as "Operator complaints are known to be inflated by industrial unrest, so it takes a laboratory study to find out what differences, if any, there are between the use of word processors and typewriters".

To this should be added that ergonomists from the viewpoint of the learned society are generalists, and that their broad-spectrum approaches sometimes do not fit in with the scientific rigor of more narrow specialists. An account of these conflicting views is given in a recent symposium report from the US National Research Council (Brown et al., 1982). The theme of the report is that there are *abundant indications* of VDT work-place problems, but that *true scientific proofs are lacking*. The NRC rapporteurs write that "even well-designed field studies can provide only limited information"; the research effort should therefore focus on strictly controlled multivariate full-scale experiments over many years and should include comparisons of different traditional office tasks with different VDT tasks.

There are, to use an American expression, differences in the problem conceptions between Wall Street and Main Street. In the present context this can be re-phrased to "The universities have faculties — and the society has problems."

Field studies from all over the world show that prolonged routine VDT work elicits operator complaints. Figure 1 summarizes the result of the first Swedish survey. It was carried out as an in-house investigation at the Skandia Insurance Company in 1976, and tapped the percentage of its personnel relating their discomfort/ailments to the VDT work *per se*. Several investigations have since then been carried out in Sweden, and in particular with regard to the high percentage of visual/ocular discomfort shown in the Skandia investigation. The results in Figure 2 include the Skandia investigation among later Swedish investigations. Figure 2 clearly shows that the number of daily VDT hours have a bearing on the frequency of the operators' statements on experienced visual/ocular discomfort.

Figure 1

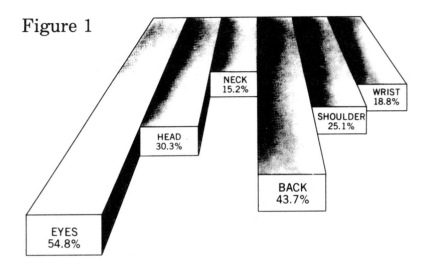

NECK 15.2%

WRIST 18.8%

SHOULDER 25.1%

HEAD 30.3%

BACK 43.7%

EYES 54.8%

As elaborated in the 1976 review on "Office Computerization," the ophthalmologic status of the operators also has a bearing on the frequency of visual/ocular discomfort; this has for example been confirmed by the medical department of IBM France (Gilet et al., 1978). Probably the most careful investigation on such a relationship has been performed for another demanding visual task —microscope work—and the investigators (Soderberg et al., 1978) were able to prove without doubts that for fusion inadequacy, uncorrected astigmatism, and nonoptimal refraction, operator complaints increased with time at the microscope.

Furthermore, Gunnarsson and Östberg (1976) have shown that the visual/ocular discomfort claims also are dependent on the type of VDT task performed. Time and again, and all over the world, similar findings have been reported, and we now know for sure that the number of complaints from VDT operators tend to increase with increased degrees of such negative job design features as monotony, fragmentation, pacing, control, repetitiveness, social isolation and job insecurity.

Figure 2

Visual Strain in VDT Work

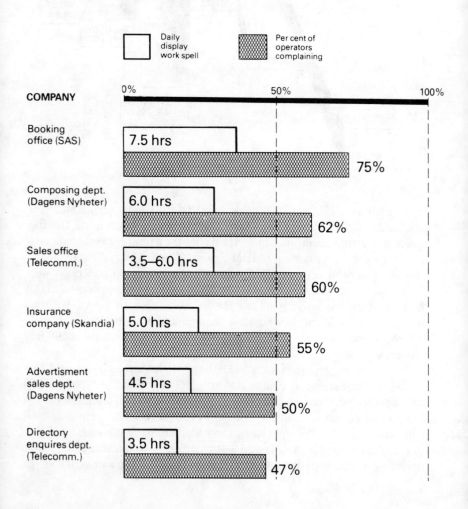

Socio-technical Labor Contracts

In Sweden, the first handbook on the design of VDT workplaces was published for a governmental agency (Ostberg et al., 1974) and since then in Sweden alone there have been a dozen followers. Internationally, **The VDT Manual** (Cakir et al., 1979) is perhaps the most well known example in the handbook genre.

Handbooks are fine, provided they are sound and consulted by people who are willing, able and influential enough to act accordingly. Certain handbook advice might qualify as firm design criteria and will then have a greater impact if issued in the form of national or international guidelines/standards. A third way of governing the design and use of VDTs would be to publish national safety and health regulations, in which reference can also be made to the design of the VDT job *per se*. Again Sweden was the forerunner inasmuch as the regulations of the Swedish NBOSH (1978) are binding and contain the following statement on VDT job design:

> If eye fatigue or visual discomfort tends to develop, the work must be organized in such a way that the employee can intermittently be given periods of rest or work involving more conventional visual requirements.

A more far-reaching statement, but without legislative power, is the following set of recommendations from the US NIOSH (1981):

> Based on our concern about potential chronic effects on the visual system and musculature and prolonged psychological distress, we recommend the following work-rest breaks for VDT operators:
>
> 1. A 15-minute work-rest break should be taken after two hours of continuous VDT work for operators under moderate visual demands and/or work load.
> 2. A 15-minute work-rest break should be taken after one hour of continuous VDT work for operators under high visual

demands, high work load and/or those engaged in repetitive
work tasks.

Yet further goes the Norwegian NBOSH (1981), but the following
formulation in the proposed regulation has been criticized by industry
and might be weakened in the final version of the regulation:

> If the VDT work consists of data-entry tasks or other routine
> VDT tasks, the work spell at the VDT shall not have a dura-
> tion exceeding 50 per cent of the total working hours. Further-
> more, the VDT work spell should not exceed two hours
> without a short rest pause.

> The task performed during the remaining part of the working
> day should as much as possible be related to the task at the
> VDT.

The above examples of (attempted) regulations of the design of VDT
jobs show that national safety and health agencies are sensitive to the
goings-on at the office floor. As was discussed in the previous section,
the learned society (and industry) might challenge the facts upon which
these regulatory statements are founded.

- How is eye fatigue defined?
- What constitutes moderate visual demands?
- Why the rule 15 minutes per one hour? Etc.

In fact, the real world is so complex that far-reaching general regulatory statements on job design will always run the risk of being ques-
tioned on their scientific foundations and validity for a specific VDT
application. In the final analysis the job design aspects of person-computer interaction boil down to the worker-management interaction of
the computerized production system. Hence the dilemma can not be
resolved by increased research effort only. Regulatory actions must
therefore be supplemental by rights given to the weaker part—the
worker side—to have a say in the design, implementation and operation
of computer systems.

The Scandinavian countries benefit from a very high degree of union-ization, even for office workers within all production and governmental sectors. It is feasible that this explains why the Scandinavian countries now can show up a great variety of socio-technical labor contracts. Elsewhere I have looked upon the use of such contracts from a Swedish salaried employee trade union view (Ostberg, 1982) and showed how this fits in with the Swedish society's tradition in the industrial relations area. An outside view has recently been provided by Deutsch (1982), from whose report the following is cited:

> A major contribution which Scandinavian unions and re-searchers have made is to address the work environment in holistic terms. Contrary to the tendency in the US to limit discussion to traditional job safety and health factors or phys-ical and chemical hazards, the Scandinavians have understood that the psychological hazards of job stress and the nature of work relations are integrally tied to one another. As a result, the introduction of new technology into the workplace is ap-proached as part of a larger set of worker and union rights to constantly improve the workplace.

The International Federation of Information Processors (IFIP) held a conference in Riva del Sole, Italy, September 20-24, 1982, and the theme of the conference was **System Design for, with and by the Users.** That is also a most appropriate denotation for capturing current Scandinavian attitudes towards new technology. But it is not just atti-tudes. At all society levels it seethes of activities, which often have been initiated by unions. Even as regards research activities, the un-ions hereby do affect the end results and end policies. These are some examples from Sweden:

- The Government's Datadelegation is actively working to restore "The Swedish Model" and create tools, protocols, knowledge and resources for the furthering of co-determi-nation and promotion of user-friendly application of new technology. All political parties and major labor market organizations are represented in the Datadelegation. (In Sweden, major labor market organizations refers to the national bargaining federations for employees and employers, respectively, in the private, government and local government sectors.)

- The National Research Council has set up a committee with delegates from research institutions and labor market organizations, the result of which is a proposal for a concerted national research programme concerning the application of new technology. Among other things, the program calls for the creation of several new university professorships "for the study of the development of the computerized society."

- The Board for Technical Development has started a five year program financing some one hundred researchers in the area of information technology. This is a significant resource allocation in a country with a population of 8.3 million people. The unions have two seats in the steering committee for the program, and have also been granted resources to be able to formulate union policies in terms of research needs.

- The Work Environment Fund has set aside 50 million kronor (equivalent to US $1.00 per capita) to allow the labor market organizations to jointly try out progressive applications of new technology. The program focuses on field experiments and development of work organizations in new technology settings.

- The Centre for Working Life has quite a few ongoing research projects in which researchers and local and central union representatives work together to find new ways to capture, express and carry the workforce views on the design, implementation and operation of computer systems.

- The major labor market organizations have formulated explicit data policies/programs and have issued films, books and training courses to promote efficient and user-friendly applications of new technology. In schools of all levels, curricula dealing with computer technology always render an account of these new technology policies.

- The Utopia Project (1982) is a Nordic research project on organized labor development of and training in computer technology — particularly with regard to text and image processing in the graphic industry, but also in regard to office automation. It is a model project wherein researchers in close collaboration with union representatives aim at designing a trade union alternative production system for the graphic industry. The project is to result in a "technical success", in that it shall be competitive on the market, and yet provide real benefits for graphics workers.

What is the Message of Computers?

We used to hear that "The media is the message". That was in discussions on the impact of TV. A nation dominated by TV, all the way from how the family's daily life is formed and performed to the way politicians behave and get elected, is surely getting a "message" from the TV setting that is more important than the broadcast message from the TV set.

Similarly it is becoming acknowledged that the introduction of home and school computers and computer games will have an impact on society. What is this new "message"? And at the workplace? That we do not know, but we do know that it is important.

It has, however, become obvious to a great many office workers, especially low-paid clerks that the advent of computers has meant degradation of the skill needed at the work, a shift from personal and social work interaction to impersonal and computer-tailored person-machine dialogue (or monologue), increased discomfort from the back, arms and eyes, and well-founded worry of their job security. There are, on the other hand, groups of workers, especially among the professionals, who see mostly positive changes with the computerization.

Is there one messaage for the low-paid (female) clerks and another message for the well-paid (male) professionals?

We now hear that Artificial Intelligence (AI) is coming to make all computer systems user-friendly. But how can technology *per se* create user-friendliness if the users (the workers) of computer systems are treated as unfriendly when they ask for a say in the design, implementation and operation of the systems?

We now hear that Voice Technology is coming to free the office workers from the strain of viewing VDT screens and operating VDT keyboards. But the talking and listening computers will for many years have a very limited vocabulary and an inferior pronunciation of the voice output. It is foreseeable that voice recognition systems will impose severe restrictions on the workplace design and the job design of the voice terminal operators, restrictions similar to those described above for the operators in the early OCR systems.

When typing this manuscript, a few paragraphs ago, I had to consult **Webster's New World Dictionary of the American Language**. I had to check if I should write low-paid, low paid or lowpaid. I then ran across the following explanation:

> LUDDITE, said to be after Fred Lud, a feeble-minded man who smashed two frames belonging to a Leicestershire employer (c.1779), any of a group of workers in England between 1811 and 1816 who smashed new labor-saving textile machinery in protest against reduced wages and unemployment attributed to its introduction.

That does in no way seem to have been a feeble-minded thing to do in those days! But the times they are achanging and there are no longer any Luddites or Luddite minds around. Instead there is an increasing number of office workers who care about the working conditions, who are devoted to take part in the creation of brave new offices, and who are keen in working in meaningful and efficient production systems. That surely must be an asset for the employers, and it surely must be a stimulating task for researchers to help unveil, express and carry through that latent power.

References

Boivie, P.E., & Ostberg, O., **Programme of Data Policy for The Central Organization of Salaried Employees in Sweden (TCO).** Proceedings of the International Federation for Information Processing (IFIP) Conference on Systems Design For, With and By the Users, Riva del Sole, Italy, September 20-24, 1982.

Brown, B.S., Dismukes, K., & Rinalducci, E.R., "Video Display Terminals and Vision of Workers, Summary and Overview of a Symposium," **Behaviour and Information Technology,** 121-140, 1, 1982.

Cakir, A., Hart, D.J., & Stewart, T.F.M., **The VDT Manual.** Darmstadt: INCA-FIEJ Research Association, 1979.

Deutsch, S., "Unions and Technological Change, International Perspectives," In D. Kennedy, C. Craypo, & M. Lehman (Eds.), **Labor and Technology: Union Responses to Changing Environments.** University Park, PA: Pennsylvania State University, 1982.

Felmann, Th., Breuninger, U., Gierer, R., & Grandjean, E., "An Ergonomic Evaluation of VDTs," **Behaviour and Information Technology,** 69-80, 1, 1982.

Gilet, A., Grall, Y., Keller, J., & Vienot, P.A., "Le Travail sur Terminal a Ecran," **Archives des Maladies Professionelles, de Medecine du Travail et de Securite Sociale,** 357-373, 39, 1978.

Gunnarsson, E., & Östberg, O., **The Physical and Psychological Working Environment in a Terminal-based Computer Storage and Retrieval System.** Stockholm: Swedish NBOSH, 1977. (Investigation Report No. 35).

Hultgren, G.V., & Knave, B., "Discomfort Glare and Disturbances from Light Relections in an Office Landscape with CRT Display Terminals," **Applied Ergonomics,** 2-8, 5, 1974.

Mackay, C., **Human Factors in the Development of a Document Correction System.** Loughborough, GB: Loughborough University of Technology, 1971. (M.Sc. Project Report in Ergonomics).

Norwegian NBOSH, **Proposal for Regulations and Guidelines for Display Terminal Workplaces.** (In Norwegian). Oslo: National Board of Occupational Safety & Health, 1981.

Östberg, O., "Office Computerization in Sweden: Worker Participation, Workplace Design Considerations, and the Reduction of Visual Strain," In B. Shackel (Ed.), **Man-Computer Interaction: Human Factors Aspects of Computers & People.** Alphen aan den Rijn, The Netherlands: Sijthoff & Noordhoff, 1981. (Proceedings of a NATO Symposium held in Mato, Greece, 1976).

Östberg, O., "The Empirics of Specialization and Division of Labor among Swedish Salaried Employees—A Trade Union View on the Technical Development," **Proceedings of the International Symposium on "Division of Labor, Specialization and Technical Development, Linkoping, Sweden, June 7-11, 1982.** (Stockholm, ERU, Department of Industry).

Östberg, O., Damadaran, L., Mackay, C.J., Stewart, T.F.M., & Stone, P.T., **Terminal Functions and Terminal Workplaces.** (In Swedish). Stockholm: National Agency of Administrative Development, 1974.

Soderberg, I., Calissendorff, B., Elofsson, S., Knave, B., & Nyman, K.G., "Microscope Work. I: Investigation of Visual Strain Experienced by Microscope Operators at an Electronic Plant," **Work and Health,** No. 16, 1978. (Swedish NBOSH).

Swedish CIS. **Ergonomics—Requirements in Information Processing—Image Quality on Cathode Ray Tube (CRT) Based Visual Display Units for Text Presentation in Office Environment.** (Draft 1982-07-12; for ISO). Stockholm: Standards Commission, 1982.

Swedish NBOSH. **Reading of Display Screens. NBOSH Directive No. 16.** (In Swedish). Stockholm: National Board of Occupational Safety & Health, 1978.

The Utopia Project. On Training, Technology, and Products Viewed from the Quality of Work Perspective. Stockholm: Centre for Working Life, 1982.

US NIOSH. **Potential Health Hazards of Video Display Terminals.** Cincinnati, OH: National Institute for Occupational Safety & Health, 1981.

Labor Legislation in Norway:
Its Application to the Introduction of New Technology

Lisbet Hjort

Directorate of Organization and Management, Norway

In Norway rules concerning the introduction and use of Video Display Terminals (VDTs) were suggested in 1981, causing considerable comment and debate. The following is an outline of the legislative basis for proposing such rules, the administrative apparatus for enforcing rules mandated by legislation, and a little about the rules themselves.

The legislative basis for issuing any rules or regulations concerning work environment or workers' protection in Norway is the **Act Relating to Workers Protection and Working Environment of February 4, 1977**. The main function of the Act is to set out goals upon which there already exists a high degree of consensus in the Norwegian society. It gives *information* as to the rights and duties of both employers and employees, producers and vendors. Only very occasionally is it used as a basis for laying claims to economic compensation, or for criminal proceedings. The Act mandates to the Directorate of Labour Inspection the right to issue regulations pertaining to specific sections of the Act.

The definition of work environment in the act covers:

- Technology
- Work Organization
- Working Hours
- Wage Systems

This is quite comprehensive, and the Act covers both the separate factors as well as the totality of the factors influencing the work situation. The Act is primarily concerned with developing the work environment so that it is harmful to neither the physical nor the mental health and well-being of the workers. It specifies that the work shall be arranged so that it offers possibilities of personal and professional development through learning and self-determination on the job.

The Act is designed primarily to *prevent* ill health from developing, through the use and arrangement of technology, work organization, working hours, and wage systems. It also concerns the basic human and democratic right to determine about one's self-determination, at work as well as in private, and in this way the Act is unique as far as work environment legislation goes.

Enforcement and Representation Mechanisms

Before going into details about how the law applies to the introduction of new technology, let me briefly explain the enforcing agencies. First, keep in mind that Norway is a long country (about 2,000 kilometers long) and is sparsely populated. We are a population of about 4.1 million inhabitants, with a workforce of about 1.7 million, approximately 190,000 of whom are engaged in office work. About 40,000 people use computers or VDTs daily; only about 5% of these, less than 10,000 people, do data entry work of the monotonous and intensive kind. This means that it is not too difficult to monitor and oversee working life in Norway.

The governmental body that enforces the Act is the Directorate of Labour Inspection. (Administratively this agency falls under the Ministry of Local Government and Labour.) The Labour Inspection as a whole employs about 450 people, of whom 150 are employed on the national level in the Directorate of Labour Inspection. This Directorate explains the laws, settles disputes, and issues rules and regulations pertaining to the Act on work environment.

There are also local Labour Inspection offices, comprising 12 district offices and 85 local offices, employing about 350 persons. The local offices are manned by experts such as engineers, physicians, industrial hygienists and physical therapists, as well as by inspectors with broad experience in working life. These inspectors undergo a five-week training program before starting their jobs.

Within individual enterprises, the law requires that where five or more are employed there shall be elected (by the employees) safety delegates. In workplaces employing 20 or more, a safety committee may be set up. In workplaces of 50 or more, the safety committee is mandatory. A safety committee consists of representatives of the employees and of management in equal numbers. The employees' representatives are elected by and among the employees themselves. Some workplaces have collective bargaining agreements that also provide for data shop stewards.

Some 50 to 60% of the working population is unionized. This means that in many places you will have union representatives, and these representatives often will be on the safety committees as well.

Both safety delegates and members of the safety committees are given a basic training of 40 hours in matters concerning work environment, as required by the Act. This training is given during work hours, paid for by the employer.

The Labour Inspectorate works through these elected bodies in enterprises. The inspectors may order the employer to comply with the law in all matters concerning technology, work organization, working hours, and wage systems. Both employers and employees may, and do, call in the local inspectors. The basis for giving orders of compliance need not be necessarily the existence of medical proof of harmful working conditions, or proof that threshold limits have been exceeded.

Many harmful environment factors will not result in illness, or may not be visible or liable to measurement. Examples include authoritarian management, highly monitored or tightly controlled jobs, etc. To a large degree the inspector must rely on his own knowledge and judgement, and that of the workers.

Limiting Intensive Work at VDTs

Section 12 of the law served as the basis for rules concerning the use of VDTs. This section specifies that technology, work organization, working hours, and wage systems shall not place undue physical or mental strain on workers. By *technology* we mean processes, machine systems, electronic data processing systems, tools, materials and other physical and environmental factors, such as the room that you work in or the building. *Work organization* refers to the distribution of power and responsibility, work instructions, the content of work, relations between jobs in departments. *Working hours* concern all local regulations about working time, breaks, shift-work, etc. And *wage systems* concern the rules and routines for estimating and paying wages, although not the level of wages.

Subsection 3 of this section covers the introduction of all data-based systems, including word processors and the like. (In fact it covers all systems for planning and controlling work, whether or not they are data-based.)

Suffice it to say that the Labour Inspection considered that issuing regulations covering this type of technology might be a means to prevent ill effects and unsatisfactory work arrangements. This seemed particularly important because those most adversely affected by the new technology often were not organized and not highly skilled, and needed rules that would explain what the law could be used for in their work situation. Many women workers are included in these categories.

The Labour Inspectorate created an advisory group consisting of both L.I. personnel and research workers. This group suggested the issuance of binding rules covering:

- Technical equipment
- Use and positioning of the equipment
- Arrangement and content of work
- Training
- Eye tests

These matters generally are not covered by data agreements.

The rules also covered work periods, the initial suggestion being that no person doing monotonous work at VDTs should do so for more than 50% of his or her daily working hours, be that a part-time or full-time job.

The rules also covered ergonomic matters such as chairs, tables, etc. The rules demanded eye tests at regular intervals and stated the right to have free glasses for doing VDT work for anyone needing them. This last part has already been enforced in the entire public sector in Norway.

The ensuing debate centered mainly on the suggested limitation of intensive, monotonous work to 50% of the work hours. Managers were worried about a decrease in productivity; vendors and producers were afraid of both having their products declared obsolete and that managers would hesitate to install VDTs. Most unions were positive, but in some workplaces they worried that strict rules would limit the areas of self-determination at work. The unions also wanted more detailed rules, particularly about the technology.

An alternative rule of limiting intensive VDT work to four hours a day would eliminate the problem of limiting what was already part-time work. On the other hand, the unions agreed, such a limit might have the consequences that all data-registration and other intensive VDT work would be offered as four-hours' jobs.

The revised suggested rules presently under consideration contain no such restrictions. Instead they seek to prohibit the creation of new data entry jobs that are intensive, i.e. monotonous, repetitive, highly-monitored jobs, and recommends local bargaining about possible limitations on existing monotonous work.

The fate of these suggested rules is uncertain at the moment, for we also have a conservative government. In the meantime, however, many workplaces both in the public and private sectors have used the proposed rules as a basis for bargaining, and have arrived at agreements covering working time at VDTs. So I'm happy to relate that in reality these rules have already had some impact on a large part of Norwegian working life.

In addition, there has been a great deal of interest from other countries. We have received many inquiries, and heard many reports of other countries working with similar legislation, and of labor unions seeking to obtain agreements on the organization of work along the same lines.

Planning for the Introduction of New Technology

Having reviewed the legislative basis for proposing rules on the use of VDTs, let me go further into the question of codetermination in the process of introducing the technology.

Subsection 12.3 demands advance notice, training and the right to influence decisions concerning the introduction or change of systems for planning and controlling work. Advance notice means that the workers shall be notified at the earliest possible moment—before any decisions are made.

Training shall give insight both into the actual systems and in the use of the technology. It should also give insight in the processes of project work, organization analysis, etc.

Participation and codetermination cover many factors:

- deciding about pilot project/main project
- the setting of goals
- system design
- designing job routines/content
- choosing equipment
- arranging the workplace
- analysis and evaluation of consequences

The prerequisites for participation are:

(1) *Time,* for discussion, meetings, training and referring back to the other workers, for analysis of own work as a basis for evaluating to what purpose the technology can be used, and its consequences.
(2) *Information,* understandable and given in advance on all relevant matters.

(3) *Bargaining experience*, preferably an apparatus through which matters of conflict can be handled (union, work environment committee with deciding powers).

In the planning process, in the project group, there are several issues to be analyzed. The following issues all relate to section 12 of the Act.

What will the consequences for the jobs and the work organization with regard to:

- decisionmaking and self-determination
- content of work
- variation in tasks
- connection between tasks
- opportunity for development of personal and professional skills
- cooperation and contact with coworkers
- relationship between jobs
- possibilities of influencing features of the system (stopping, re-programming, etc.)
- system design (fit to own method of work, workpace and pattern)
- need for training and further education in EDP/system design

Other considerations include: who shall be given training? (those directly influenced and workers' representatives); when? before starting projects and when use of new system is imminent); and how? (preferably closely connected to the actual work situation).

I have concentrated here on the workers' right to codetermination in the process of planning for the introduction of new technology. I think that matters concerning ergonomics (glare, static electricity, etc.) are not really the central issue in Norway; in most workplaces serious work is done to solve these problems.

The real problem, as we see it, is the content of work. Ergonomics make a boring or stressful job only marginally better. I believe that it is through codetermination that it will be possible to avoid the creation of monotonous jobs, and to develop jobs that are more interesting and make a more productive and creative use of this new technology.

Occupational Health and the Design of Work

Kari Thoresen
Norwegian Computing Center, Norway

How does the work itself, and the way that is is organized, affect occupational health?

We already know that ergonomics is important, and we know quite a lot about what kind of equipment we should buy and how the work station should be designed from an ergonomical point of view. But we know very little about how the organization of work influences occupational health. Although we have a great many suspicions about this interrelationship, there are very few hard facts to back up our knowledge on this point.

I believe that now is the time to direct our attention more towards work organization than ergonomics. To illustrate my point, I will cite some of the results from a study we conducted a couple of years ago on the working conditions in several computerized offices. These offices were: data entry departments, a text processing center, a travel agency, a social security office, and order entry, i.e. sales by telephone.

This was a small study that included only 113 persons. It covered a variety of job situations, even though all were clerical, on the lower part of the job hierarchy, and they all used VDTs in their jobs. Some of them were highly specialized. They had only a very few tasks to perform, and spent most of their working day with the VDT.

Another group was less specialized. They had several tasks to perform, and they used the VDTs mostly as a tool for problem-solving and information retrieval. As a group they spent less than two hours in total with the VDT each day.

We were interested in the differences between these two groups with regard to physical ailments, and we asked about eye fatigue, muscular pains, headaches, etc. These are the usual questions that you ask about physical ailments in computerized offices.

Following are the results for both groups. (See Figure 1.) The figures show the percentages of the sample which had some kind of symptoms every day, or several times a week. As you see, the results for the least specialized group (the left bar on each chart) were not bad, really. The eyes are about 27%; 10% often have trouble with their neck muscles; 8% with their shoulders; and headaches, 18%; and back problems, 4%.

The bars on the right show the results for the specialized group. You see that the increase in percentages having some kind of trouble is very large. It's almost doubling for the eyes. For the neck it's more than four times as many who have problems; the same with the shoulders. With headaches, we see a doubling again. Back and wrists were not that important really; the figures were smaller. And personally, I doubt if this difference is related to the equipment. In fact, the ergonomics of the VDTs and the work station in the first group was, on the whole, better for the specialized group. To me it's rather obvious: it's the work itself that we should examine.

The specialized group all had routine work, sometimes monotonous, with little job discretion. And this trend toward more fragmented and more controlled work is not the consequence of the new technology. It's a long development which has its roots back in the beginning of the century when Taylorism became the dominant trend. A new technology is merely the last tool in this process, so that the different occupational health problems that we now see should be viewed as the social costs of this development. Unless we reorganize work, we will never be able to reduce these social costs.

Ergonomics, in other words, are only the beginning. Reducing the working time on VDTs is one thing. But the basic organization of work

Figure 1: Relation between total time in front of the screen each day and the percentage troubled by physical ailments daily or several times a week.

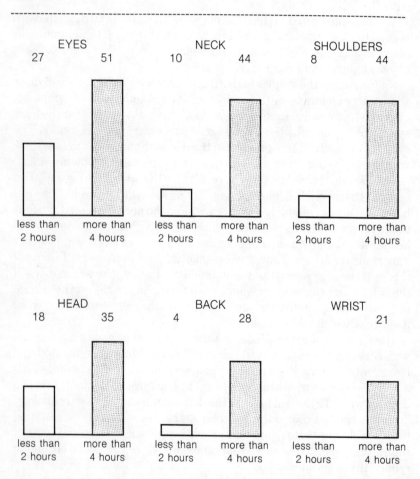

is much more than that. As Lisbet Hjort has pointed out, a good work organization includes not only variational work, but also allowances for job discretion, opportunities for contact with co-workers, and the potential for learning and growth.

Reducing the time with the VDT does not guarantee any of these qualities. It's purely a technical measure. But the possibility of contact with your colleagues—that's one of the basic needs just for the office to be able to function. It's also a very important need for office workers and other workers to get together to talk about their problems and discuss strategies.

The reason we advocate reduced time with the VDT is only partly because of the occupational health aspect. This demand also could be an impulse to start thinking about new ways of organizing the work. If we do not succeed in this process, I believe that we will have another problem very soon—the question of who will be employed in the computerized office. Here I am not thinking about the skills and education required, but rather about who can stand the physical and psychological strains of some of these jobs.

Are we creating jobs, for instance, that can be handled only by young, healthy people with perfect eyes? I am afraid that we may see a new period where people are selected more on the basis of their ability to take physical and mental strain than their other qualifications. In fact I have listened to several discussions between physicians about how to select people for VDT work. Some even mentioned biopsies to pick people with the right muscular structure for VDTs. I don't know how serious they were, but this was mentioned.

Some years ago, the **EDP Analyzer**, a computer newsletter, had some interesting information about the qualifications of a text processing operator. She should be: prepared to work with machines instead of people; she should like working with small details; she should accept sitting at her work station for long periods; she should be able to work in a noisy environment; and used to detailed monitoring and correction of her work.

To us, such selection criteria are not only unacceptable, but also illegal according to our working environment act. That does not mean that everybody should have the right to work with VDTs. In many cases, it will be better to offer people who can't work with them other types of work, of course. But I think there is a world of difference between using selection as a principle, or just as a last resort.

An Issue of Respect:
Women Workers Demand Healthy and Safe Offices
Mary Mitchell
Boston 9 to 5

9to5, National Association of Working Women, has been doing a great deal about office health and safety, on a national level and locally through its Boston chapter. Through surveys, interviews, reports and Congressional testimony, 9to5 has found that women working on VDTs in Boston and across the nation are suffering from ill health as a result of working on these machines.

More importantly, these working women usually are aware of the connection between their jobs and their physical ailments. Personal stories repeat familiar refrains. We leave our office with headaches at the end of each day. Our eyesight deteriorates. Eyeglasses are needed where none were before. Stronger prescriptions are required. We are threatened with dismissal if our production falls under quota. Nervous stomachs, shakiness, skin rashes, and sore muscles are commonplace.

9to5's survey of office workers compiled in 1981 clearly showed that health complaints increased dramatically as VDT use comprises a greater proportion of one's job.

Not only are office workers aware of the connection between their jobs and their health, but they are also capable of analyzing a bad situation and pursuing practical solutions to it. Most clerical workers in

Boston are not unionized, and depend on 9to5 for information and advice about automation. Armed with this information, our contacts have educated not only themselves, but also their co-workers and their supervisors. Office workers have successfully achieved solutions to reduce glare, moderate lighting level, and reduce noise levels in their offices. A group of typesetters, for example, rearranged their office floor plan to better accommodate the VDTs. A pregnant woman persuaded her company to purchase a lead apron to protect her unborn child from low-level radiation.

More than anyone else in the workplace, 9to5 has found that office workers themselves are the experts on office automation. Their supervisors and managers sorely need an education about how office automation can be used both safely and productively in the office. Computer manufacturers are selling their equipment without so much as a mention about the safe use of their product. There is a real need among office workers for information about how to evaluate specific equipment.

At 9to5 we receive frequent inquiries from women who are already working on VDTs, and want to know, for instance, if their headaches or eyestrain could possibly be due to the design of their machine. And we hear from women who know their office will be automating and want to voice their preferences before their machines are installed. To fill this need, Boston 9to5 launched an in-depth evaluation of word processors on the market. We identified those design features we felt were most important to the users' health and safety. We proceeded to meet with those manufacturers who agreed to participate to view and evaluate their product.

Out of this project came the report, **The Human Factor**, which provides information about specific equipment that would otherwise be difficult for an office worker to obtain. Armed with this information, she can evaluate any machine, comparing it to those models listed here, and make an intelligent recommendation for improvement to her employer.

The Human Factor is an important first step in changing the automated office environment, but even if all manufacturers complied with our recommendations the equipment could still be used to regulate and de-humanize office workers. 9to5 has identified offices that are virtual information assembly lines. VDT operators are under the constant pressure of production quotas, upon which not only their raises, but their very employment is based. Their machines record every keystroke and every pause. If a machine is left untended for more than a few minutes in some companies, an alarm will sound, or their screen will go dead. In one Boston company, the first thing an operator sees on her screen as she begins her day's work is the greeting: "Are you ready to be bored again?".

A ten year veteran of CRT operations confided to a co-worker: "As soon as I sit down at that machine in the morning, I feel like I am going to cry." In other offices, the tyranny is more subtle, but it's still there. A secretary with a new word processor suddenly finds herself swamped with more typing than ever before. As she struggles to master the complexities of the new machine, she meets the frustration of her supervisors, who believe that producing an error-free document is an easy matter of simply pressing a button. A supervisor thus ignores the intelligence and skill required to run a word processor.

A secretary noticed that when the boss brings new clients through the office, he'll point right to her, working on the word processor, and say: "Here we have our wonderful new Lexitron," and then move right on. "He doesn't bother to introduce me, just the machine."

9to5 has worked for nearly ten years under the motto "Rights and Respect for Women Office Workers." We are battling the misconception that office work is unskilled and insignificant. Anyone who works in an office knows that we are important. Without us, communication comes to a halt, and information becomes inaccessible. The processing of cash receipts and disbursements stops without clerical support.

The issues surrounding office automation are fundamental issues of respect. Certainly the lack of respect is evident in the experiences of the office workers I have referred to. Those who plan for the implementation of automation can show their respect for us by designing systems that will free office workers from monotonous and boring tasks, and by allowing for the full utilization of our skills and intelligence. This technology does have the capability of freeing us from office drudgery. I hope we have the sense to utilize that capability to the fullest.

An Overview of NIOSH Research on Clerical Workers

Barbara Cohen
Research Psychologist
National Institute for Occupational Safety and Health

The National Institute of Occupational Safety and Health was created "to assure that every man and woman has a safe and healthful working environment," and "to preserve our human resources." Those are quotes from the mandate that created NIOSH. A large segment of our U.S. working population, 18 to 20 million clerical workers, are just now getting some deserved attention, and they are going to be the focus of my project for preserving our human resources for the next couple of years.

The need for research on this occupational group has been illustrated by several recent studies, notably the San Francisco NIOSH VDT study that has been cited in this conference. I would like to describe that study a little bit, as well as discuss current NIOSH research of computerized offices—what NIOSH is doing now and what it is planning in the near future.

We have heard a good deal about the unions' lack of power in the U.S. compared to our European and Scandinavian counterparts. But the NIOSH San Francisco study was initiated by unions, by a consortium of five unions, because of the many reports and complaints of sore eyes, headaches, backaches and similar ailments on the part of workers. The unions requested a health hazard evaluation, and there followed a comprehensive investigation of VDT operations in five different work sites. A variety of tests were carried out, including: (1) an industrial hygiene sampling of air contaminants; (2) an ergonomic evaluation; (3) radiation measurements. Fourth, reports of physical health symptoms were investigated. And fifth, an evaluation of stress and strain as reported by the workers was undertaken.

There were five work sites: three newspapers, a newspaper agency, and an insurance company. They were in the midst of changing over to VDTs, so this provided an excellent opportunity to study two groups of clerical workers. One group had the same jobs except that they used traditional office equipment, such as electric typewriters, to perform their tasks; this was the control group. The other group had the same tasks except that they used VDTs to perform them. The clerical VDT workers experienced significantly more physical complaints, and perceived more job stress and strain, such as feeling much more work pressure, compared to their fellow workers in the same organization doing the same work except without the VDTs.

Well, if it were not for a third group of VDT workers included in the study, we might have assumed that it was the VDT machines themselves that were causing all these problems. The third group consisted of reporters, editors, copy editors and printers; for the lack of a better term we called them the professionals using VDTs. Although they spent the same amount of time as the other VDT operators looking at their terminals, they experienced far less physical complaints and far less job stress.

A clear pattern emerged throughout this study. On every single scale of stress, physical or emotional or psycho-social, the clerical VDT operators scored the highest in terms of stress. The professional VDT operators scored the least in stress and strain, and the clerical workers not using VDTs placed somewhere in between. This suggests that it was not just the VDT that was contributing to job stress; there had to be other factors such as organizational factors and job content.

Let me quickly summarize the results. When we looked at job content we found that the clerical workers' jobs involved rigid work procedures, high production standards, constant pressure for performance, little control over their own tasks, and minimal participation or identification or satisfaction with their end product. The professionals, on the other hand, had a great deal of flexibility over how they would do their work and how they would meet their deadlines. They also were able to utilize their education and creativity, allowing them to experience a great deal of pride and satisfaction in their end product.

Clearly, ergonomics and industrial hygiene factors are important in office workers' health and safety, and in no way do I minimize their importance. But it's my opinion that the most serious health threat to office workers comes from the chronic, daily psycho-social stresses that impact on many clerical workers. These factors include: working relationships with fellow workers and supervisors; participating in decisions that affect their own work; having some control over their own job; and having some kind of status, some way that self-esteem can be maintained on the job.

Right now I am designing a pilot study to characterize and define just what the stressors are. What makes up the cumulative stress that affects the health of clerical workers? Also, I hope to discover what can be done about changing or alleviating stress and strain. This study should be under way in 1983 and will take about three years. It will be a field study carried out at two different work sites.

Another field study being conducted through contract with NIOSH, by the University of Wisconsin, concerns state employees. Preliminary data from this study confirmed higher musculo-skeletal and visual complaints are present in VDT workers than in clerical workers not using VDTs—but both groups had equivalent levels of job stress. These results are based on preliminary data analyses; therefore they are merely indicators. However, it seems to demonstrate that job stress is more related to job content and organizational factors than to ergonomic factors.

Another field study at NIOSH, involving federal government employees, is looking at the relationship between ergonomic deficiencies and high levels of psychological disorders.

Several lab studies also are in progress. In one of the NIOSH labs, the posture of VDT operators is being evaluated. A preview of the results indicates that we don't sit the way the books say we do, or say that we should; and that many of us do not adjust our furniture even when is is easily adjustable. A follow-up study is going to elaborate on this posture/ergonomics study, and will involve EMG measurements to look at the impact on muscles that are imposed by different posture positions used by workers.

A fifth lab study slated for this year will examine the effects of glare and lighting. This will be carried out by Dr. Olov Östberg, our visiting scientist from Sweden, along with another visiting scientist, Dr. Marv Dainoff from Miami University, Oxford, Ohio.

And sixth is a series of studies of job demands, psychological stresses, and lack of job control. This is being planned for laboratory study with a monitoring of heart-rate, blood pressure, and respiration rate.

There are also a number of studies under way concerning basic visual processes which are being sponsored by NIOSH at different universities. At New York University, Dr. Jacob Pas, a bio-medical engineer, will study changes in subjects' pupillary responses while viewing the VDT. These will be dynamic measurements taken while people are working at their own work-site.

Finally, there are some very interesting visual tests going on. Let me conclude by mentioning that NIOSH itself is doing an in-house longitudinal study of their own employees. One hundred employees who will be getting VDTs have received opthomological exams and optometric exams. They will receive these tests each year for five years to measure whether or not there is any kind of chronic stress effect.

These and other studies that are being conducted represent a good start for the vast amount that remains to be learned in order to promote and maintain the well-being of office workers.

Health Hazards in the Computerized Office[*]

Jeanne M. Stellman and Mary Sue Henifin
Women's Occupational Health Resource Center
Columbia University

It is evident from comments and data presented at this conference that there are a multitude of psychological and physiological implications of the computerization of office work and of the equipment used to carry out the automation process. Automation does not take place in a vacuum but rather in the context of the automation process in the existing office environment. In this paper we consider typical health hazards that can be found in the office environment which can be expected to exacerbate any adverse effect associated with the introduction and use of computerized equipment. We also discuss the difficulties of recognizing and elucidating more fully the nature of the health hazards of office work.

---

[*] From a presentation by Ms. Mary Sue Henifin at the **International Conference on Office Work & New Technology**, and from **Office Health and Safety** (working title) by Jeanne M. Stellman and Mary Sue Henifin, Pantheon, N.Y. (in press).

The Nature of Chronic Disease

Despite the prevalence of a variety of potential low level insults to the body and the spirit in the office and the large numbers of office workers at risk for these insults, there is no disease currently known as "officeitis," nor is there likely to be one. One can explain this by considering that each of the occupational health hazards described in the Table below will usually produce a slow, subtle, insidious effect over time for which cause and effect may not be discernible except under the most rigorously controlled study conditions. For example, the low levels of ozone produced by many photocopiers and computer printers will not cause the immediate acute response associated with higher, industrial levels, but can be expected to contribute to the overall burden on the upper respiratory system and the immune system. The effects of office ozone exposure, however, will be extremely difficult to sort out for the effects of other chronic insults, such as other air pollutants, on the same organ systems and, in fact, it may be impossible statistically to design an appropriate human study.

In essence, the development of similar symptoms from many different low level causes make all chronic disease particularly difficult to understand. This difficulty is even greater when the chronic factor is one related to the workplace since the vast majority of researchers and health practitioners are not trained to recognize occupational factors and instead concentrate their research and diagnostic skills on other personal lifestyle factors such as diet, exercise and individual personality traits, usually to the exclusion of the workplace environment.

Office Design and Health and Safety

Most health and safety hazards can be tied to the overall design of the office environment. The presence or absence of walls, the size of the floor area, the proximity to windows, the area allocated to an individual, the ventilation system and the provisions for access or egress will determine the extent of auditory and visual privacy available, the quality of the air, the light available for individual tasks and the ability to design a workspace with maximal provision for fire and other safety features. There has been, unfortunately, minimal attention paid to health and safety by most designers, planners and regulators. In the Table below we summarize major factors that appear to present the most serious hazards in the office.

HAZARDS OF OFFICE & CLERICAL WORK

Hazard	Selected Sources and Explanations
Muscular aches and fatigue	Poorly designed and/or non-adjustable chairs, workstations, and video display terminal components; static body positions at work stations or tasks; repetitive uncomfortable movements.
Visual fatigue and eyestrain	Non-adjustable lighting, glare, low contrast printed and written materials, highly reflecting equipment and workstation surfaces, poor air quality; demanding visual work.
Indoor air pollution	Inadequate ventilation; poorly maintained machines including ozone from photocopiers, methyl alcohol from spirit duplicators, and ammonia from blueprint machines; microorganisms in air conditioning systems; cigarette smoke, asbestos fibers in insulation or building materials; formaldehyde outgassing from pressed board and insulation.
Noise	Computer printers, photocopiers, and other office machines in general office work areas, absense of dividers and acoustical materials to block conversations, telephone and typewriter noise.

Hazard	Selected Sources and Explanations
Skin irritants	Cleaning solutions; selected adhesives, solvents, papers, and inks.
Uncomfortable temperature	Non-adjustable heating/air conditioning systems, too high or low humidity.
Fire	No sprinkler system or fire "compartmentalization," absence of fire safety plan, plastic materials that emit toxic smoke or combustion fuel load more than 15 pounds per square foot.
Unsafe conditions	Obstructed walkways and corridors, sharp edges on furniture or equipment, unbolted file cabinets, dolleys, hand trucks, rolling bases or casters unavailable for moving equipment and supplies, cluttered worksurfaces and workstations.
Psychological stress	Lack of privacy, unsupportive supervisors, isolation from co-workers, lack of control over work pace, job organization, and workstation.

Where We Go From Here

A resolution to the health and safety hazards presented here appears to involve changes in adjustability and work control. Examples of adjustability are task-oriented lighting changeable by the user, detachable keyboards on video display terminals, local control of heat and air flow, furniture that can be modified to conform to the individual needs of the person who is using the equipment. Adjustability of job design and work distribution goes hand in hand with flexibility in the design of equipment. Some examples are reallocation of work space and provision of smoking areas to accomodate both smokers and non-smokers; redistribution of work to provide variety and relief from physically demanding but also psychologically enervating routine.

The correlate of adjustability is control or the right to be involved in the adjustments of the workplace. Ongoing work by our group at Columbia** and by others has demonstrated the close correlation between the extent of control and job satisfaction, satisfaction with the work environment, irritability and other measures of stress and health. The current lack of control and adjustability is remarkable. For example, in one office that we surveyed, 80% of the occupants were not allowed to hang a picture or personalize their work area in any way. One third of the sample were unable to adjust their chairs. 83% could not adjust their lighting and 75% could not rearrange the equipment in their work areas. 80% could not control whether their personal conversations were overheard by others and could make no changes in their conditions to improve their privacy. (Further details of the study are published elsewhere.)

Our ongoing work and the findings of groups such as 9to5 demonstrate the necessity that there be a recognition of the health hazards in the total office environment and that they be taken into account as we move toward an era of total automation of the office. The interrelationships between the physical and psychological working environments must be more clearly understood.

** This work is taken from research carried out by Jeanne M. Stellman, Gloria L. Gordon, Barry R. Snow and Susan Klitzman at the School of Public Health, Columbia University, with the support of the National Institute of Mental Health Grant #3R01MH34934-02S1.

The Health Impacts of Low-Level Radiation on VDT Operators

Bob DeMatteo
Occupational Health & Safety Coordinator
Ontario Public Service Employees Union

In our union and other unions we have come across a number of problems related to Video Display Terminals (VDTs). First, there have been several clusters of adverse pregnancy outcomes among VDT operators. Second, there have been anecdotal cases of cataracts. Most of these people were too young to have cataracts, and the kind of cataracts they had were diagnosed as radiant energy induced, rather than as a result of the aging process. A third problem we have noted is skin rashes among operators while they are using VDTs. These have been reported in this country as well as in Europe, particularly in England and Scandinavia.

We have alleged that many of these health problems are due to exposure to low levels of electro-magnetic energy emitted by VDTs. There seems to be strong circumstantial evidence linking the VDTs to these particular anecdotal events.

In order to respond to these problems, we have done a lot of work to understand what was going on with VDTs. One fact is unequivocal: the VDT is a radiation emitting device, and is defined as such in Canadian law by the Radiation Emitting Devices Act. In addition, the VDT emits all forms of electro-magnetic energy now manufactured by man: extra low frequencies, radio frequencies, possibly microwaves, infra-red radiation, ultra-violet radiation, and soft X-rays. It also produces static electric fields around the operator. That would be at zero cycles per second, a stationary build-up around the sets.

The question, however, is how much is coming off the VDTs, and how much can injure you, and whether the particular levels that are found on VDTs are capable of producing the kinds of things that I pointed out at the beginning of this talk—the reproductive problems, the cataracts, the skin rashes, and possibly other kinds of effects that we are increasingly learning about.

Let me briefly describe to you what's coming off the VDT. You have a Cathode Ray Tube (CRT), which generates visual images by generating a stream of high energy electrons that strike the inner surface of the tube, which is coated with a material called phosphorous. The electron beam excites those phosphors and produces the light and visual images that you see on the screen. As that beam moves from the cathode to the anode of the set, from a negative pole to a positive pole, and hits the anode, it produces soft X-rays.

Years ago we were all concerned about the amount of X-radiation emitted from older color television sets. I remember my science and physics teachers actually irradiating things with the X-rays produced by those old sets. There's no doubt that these machines produce X-radiation. Theoretically, the evacuated tube is supposed to prevent the X-rays from going through the tube to the outer environment because of the density of the glass and the various metal alloys that are used in the glass.

Most tests on VDTs show very little X-rays, at least typically below the detection levels of the instrument used. In the U.S. the Bureau of Radiological Health did some tests on 125 VDTs, putting them under stress, and found that at least 10% did emit X-radiation in excess of the standard—way in excess of the standard. Those sets have been taken off of the market, and it was found that there were various defects in the densities of the glass, and the power supplies and the voltage regulators.

Bell Laboratories also conducted a laboratory examination, and did find some units producing excessive X-rays. Now, theoretically, there should be a margin of safety. But defects in production, in the quality of the glass and so forth, can produce machines that leak in excess of standards. Last spring IBM gave me a tour of their production plant, and I asked them how many machines they tested for X-ray emissions. They told me they test two every month because they have two manufacturers of tubes. I asked them how many machines they produced and they said 500 per day. So you also have a problem there with respect to quality control.

What about the other forms of radiation produced? Let me go back to how the VDT works. The beam is moved across the screen to produce the alpha-numeric images, and that's done through a series of electrical signals from the fly-back transformer to the deflection sytems in the sets. That usually operates at a frequency of about 15,000 cycles per second to 125,000 cycles per second—15 kilohertz to 125 kilohertz. Typically, what comes off of a VDT is a radiofrequency emission of 15 kilohertz to 125 kilohertz. This is particularly prevalent on machines with plastic cases, and whose fly-back transformers are not shielded. Low frequency radiation can come off at extremely high levels. And tests have found a prevalent signal coming off that fly-back transformer, in many cases in excess of the recommended standard.

Now, the 100 milliwatt standard for low frequency RF is supposed to be a margin of safety, but one has to ask: "What do the regulators base the standard on?" The fly-back transformer is also a source of what we call ultra-sound. Now this is not electromagnetic radiation, but this is vibration, physical vibration. And this ultrasound is at such a frequency that you could not hear it, but that doesn't mean that you could not be affected by that ultrasonic emission from the set. The Bureau of Radiological Health, I believe, found ultrasound of 45 kilohertz at something like 65 to 66 decibels being emitted from the sets. That's one of the few studies that actually looked at the ultrasound emissions.

The other source of radiation is also from the deflection systems, and here you have a basic signal going to the yoke at 30 cycles per second. That electro-magnetic signal will also produce a radio-wave, or broadcast wave coming off the sets at about 30 hertz. This is called Extra Low Frequency (ELF). The other radiation that the VDT produces on the screen itself is ultraviolet radiation. These have been shown to be practically negligible, at least below the detection limits of the instruments. The Bell Lab study by M.M. Weiss and R.C. Peterson showed that it would be no more than 1/10th of a microwatt in the far-field UV. The VDT is also a source of visible light, obviously, the only radiation you can see, and also a source of infra-red radiation, heat.

The other thing that the VDT will produce is a build-up of static charge around the unit. The machine is operating at a relatively high voltage, from 17 kilovolts up to 20 KV with some machines, and that will produce a very high static field around the set. The charge builds up both on the screen surface and in the vicinity of the operator. Those charges have been measured, and some charges have gone up to 40,000 volts per meter built up on the operator.

Let me briefly address this whole question of what's coming off the set, its level and what can cause harm, and I'll start with static electric fields. Many studies have found that there's an exchange of ions between the operator and the screen. The negative ions in front of the operator get attracted to the screen, and the positive ions from the screen get attracted to the operator.

The Norwegians feel that there is a connection between this interaction and the existence of rashes. They theorize that suspended pollutants in the air are attracted to the operator's face as a result of the charge build up. Those pollutants cause the body to react in the form of visible rashes.

There are other laboratory and human studies of this ion-exchange process that show that when you have a depletion of negative ions, it will have an effect on your body metabolism. Laboratory studies conducted by Albert Krueger at the University of California at Berkeley have shown that the progeny of rats raised in a negatively depleted environment tend to have very high mortality rates. This provides hints of the kinds of things that may be happening to operators in static electric fields. This must be viewed as being an environmental stressor because of the metabolic changes it can produce.

Extra Low Frequencies coming off VDTs have only been measured recently by the Department of National Health and Welfare in Canada. They found about 1.5 amps per meter coming off the set. At Columbia University it was found that irradiating dogs and even humans with

ELF fields at about 56 hertz, 56 cycles per second, at low power levels could alter the growth patterns in those species.

Also, there was a recent study by my union where we measured ELF fields of up to 8 milligauss, a measure of the magnetic force of the field. In Sweden, Hanson raised five generations of animals under high power lines, and the measured values were about 8 to 10 milligauss, the same levels that were found off our VDT. What he discovered in the offspring were gross morphological malformations among the animals raised in that environment.

Research studies show that exposure to ELF fields at very weak levels—less than what could be coming off the VDT—was able to disrupt the calcium ion-binding process. Recently, in the **New England Journal of Medicine**, Samuel Melham from the west coast of the U.S. reported a statistically significant increase in leukemia deaths among people who worked in occupations where they are exposed to electromagnetic fields, such as power linemen, and people working in those kinds of environments, power station operators.

Scientists are finding that the interference of the calcium ion-binding process is not a temporary phenomenon. Rashes, however, have been found to be temporary. When the operator leaves for the weekend, the rashes tend to go away.

Now, with respect to that 15 to 125 kilohertz. 1,000 volts per meter was that found by the Bureau of Radiological Health; 500 volts per meter on many, many sets were found by National Health and Welfare in Ottawa; 300 volts per meter was found in the machines used by the operators who had adverse pregnancy outcomes in our union. Very little is known about the health effects of these particular frequencies. In fact, the BRH study concludes that an empirical estimate of damage to exposure to these frequencies is impossible because there has been no biological research done in this area. However, in a very unscientific way they speculate that we should not expect any significant biological effects because these frequencies do not interact with the body. This is based not on empirical study, but on theoretical speculation.

The low levels of radiation coming off of the VDT are higher than levels that have produced significant biological change in species at certain frequencies. With respect to radiation levels from VDTs, that one thing is certain. Radiation in the area of 15 to 125 kilohertz is prevalent. More importantly, these have been shown to produce biological effects. One recent study I found showed that irradiating mice at 25 kilohertz produced 4 increases in lymphocyte mitosis in those animals. That's an important development.

Let me round up by talking about standards. The whole history of standards can be described easily. The standards are usually set too high to begin with. Then when workers die or become ill, the standards are lowered and lowered again and again. This has happened with such chemicals as vinyl chloride. This also has been the case with ionizing radiation standards. So we have to bear in mind the whole history of standard making in both the U.S. and Canada. What has been considered harmless at one point is found to be harmful later on, as a result of biological damage.

Now with respect to these machines, I think that one of the things we see happening with respect to regulatory bodies is that they are extending the presumption of innocence to an inanimate object until it is proven guilty. This is a gross perversion of the Anglo-Saxon system of jurisprudence. You just do not extend the presumption of innocence to something which is inanimate, doesn't think, contemplate, and so on. But that is what they are doing.

I think that it is careless and irresponsible on their part not to respond to the kind of biological events that are occuring among operators. They should be doing some good, qualitative empirical research. It does no good just to take the measurements off machines, apply the standard that is in question anyway, and then tell us we've got nothing to worry about.

A Union Perspective on Health Hazards of VDTs

David Eisen
Director of Research and Information
The Newspaper Guild

I will give an overview of the status of remedies in the VDT area from the standpoint of The Newspaper Guild, a union in the industry that was one of the first in which VDTs were introduced on a large scale in this country and in Canada. I'll also make some suggestions for additional research that could produce some refinement of these remedies.

There's no question that VDTs themselves have been greatly improved over the last half a dozen years. Even on this side of the Atlantic, we have VDTs that tilt and rotate, have brightness and contrast controls, with detachable keyboards and anti-glare screens and anti-glare keyboards. The trouble is that we have very few with all or most of these features, and even fewer with all of them.

Our office recently acquired a single word processor, and I inevitably was the ergonomics consultant in this proposition. We looked at six word processors, several of them with household names. Only two of them had detachable keyboards, and only one of the six could I recommend without any serious reservations. This was only a year ago.

Even a VDT perfect from an ergonomic standpoint is of little use if it stays in the workplace long past the time when the screen can be reasonably read. This is a factor in many VDT workplaces. About a year ago, Dr. Harry Snyder, a prominent researcher in the area of VDT legibility, addressed the American Industrial Hygiene Association and said something that deserves wide attention. He said that most VDT tubes should be replaced after a year's use, because their half-life is about 1500 hours, and most of them reach that by the end of the year. By that time their brightness diminishes, and if the operators try to compensate by turning up the brightness, the letters get fuzzier. He says that few manufacturers inform companies buying their tubes that after about a year they can be expected to cause visual problems if they are not replaced. And he suggested that users press manufacturers to meet European standards for those tubes.

In our shops we have tubes that go as far back as 10 years, when VDTs were first introduced, and having looked at some of those, I can tell you it is ridiculous to talk about doing anything to visually correct the situation under which those VDTs are operated.

In the area of general ergonomics, knowledge is spreading, and the availability of the equipment is improving. Two years ago, when we were first drafting the handbook that we have put out together with the Typographical Union on ergonomic measures in the VDT workplace, I was hard put to find—I finally did—one company that manufactured adjustable tables in the United States. I did not find any in Canada. There are now 8 or 10, at least, that manufacture adjustable tables. But there are very few of them installed, certainly in our industry, because they are expensive items, they don't bring in any dollars and they are very difficult to extract from management.

Chairs are a little bit more widespread. But bad chairs are very prevalent, and even adjustable chairs are not necessarily good VDT chairs. There are still far too many examples of simple four-legged, flat-footed, unadjustable, unmoveable chairs with operators breaking their backs on them with no support whatsoever.

Perhaps knowledge is greatest in the area of lighting. People know that you can't just turn on supermarket-level lighting over a VDT. And there is a glare problem. But most of the solutions are quick-fix solutions, usually glare filters. One of the first things I ever heard Dr. Michael Smith of NIOSH say was that glare should be eliminated at the source. You should take a number of other steps, principally with the lighting, and only use glare filters as a last resort. But the use of louvers or indirect lighting, the really correct way to approach the problem, is very spotty.

Let me jump to rest breaks. We have encountered the greatest resistance imaginable to this. The American Newspaper Publishers Association's spokesman at one point accused NIOSH of trying to lower productivity of American industry 25% by recommending 15-minute work breaks after one hour of very intensive VDT use. So it's not very surprising that we have only negotiated 11 rest breaks in some 200 contracts, and most of these are not adequate; they don't spell out the time or the periodicity of rest breaks.

We don't have figures for a lot of ergonomic measures. Fortunately, I recently obtained a very helpful breakdown that came from the Canadian Daily Newspaper Publishers Association in making a submission to an Ontario Task Force on the Health Hazards of Visual Display Units. Among other things, they asked their members to answer how they were responding to visual complaints, musculo-skeletal complaints, and so forth. In the area of ergonomics, among 37 newspapers, six were doing nothing; three others were doing studies but nothing else; in six cases the remedies were only in the area of lighting; in 10 other cases, only in the area of glare; in three other cases, furniture only; and in nine cases, both. But "both" might mean only glare filters and replacing chairs.

However, in one place there stood out a long list of remedies: "Glare reducing fluorescent tubes and light lenses have been installed, filters on screens, adjustable VDT pedestals, strengthened chair backs, complete station redesign and adjustable chairs and terminal stands, foot rests and drapes." The union there is the Southern Ontario Newspaper Guild, one of our most active VDT locals. Generally you'll find a correlation between union organization and action in this area.

In the area of rest breaks: We feel very strongly that rest breaks should be scheduled, not unscheduled. If they are not scheduled, they will not be taken. We have evidence of that among people who are considered professionals, newspaper editorial employees, with a great deal of workplace autonomy. But we need more research in the area of work breaks and their effect on productivity. Now even if work breaks meant a net loss in productivity, we would not hesitate to insist on them. It is the health of the employees whose work makes it possible for the companies to make vastly increased profits from these VDTs, it's their health that is at stake. Rest breaks are needed and should be taken. But even with all the smoke screens that have been created, there is every indication that work breaks have a positive effect on productivity and work performance, and we would like to see research to confirm this.

Finally, we would like to see research in three principal areas involving major health segments. The first is musculo-skeletal research. We have testimony from German researchers who worked with a thousand VDT operators that a very large percentage had to go to doctors for back treatment in one year that they were working on VDTs, and the researchers commented that permanent damage is very often the result of this kind of effect.

We would like to see epidemiological research in the area of eye damage, especially cataracts. There is only one study, among a small group of employees at the Baltimore Sun papers, about 400 employees, conducted by NIOSH. NIOSH found no significant difference between VDT operators and non-operators in the area of cataracts, but NIOSH was the first to say that this was not the final word on the subject; the average length of time worked on VDTs was too short. We also need research on long-term visual damage, something which will probably take a longitudinal study.

The third area is possibly the most important: we need an epidemiological study in the area of birth abnormalities. Many of you are aware of the eight birth defects and miscarriages in the U.S. and Canada over a period of two years. A whole new area of possible cause of this has now come to light—the area of Extremely Low Frequency radiation. Responsible scientists, knowledgeable in this area, have postulated the hypothesis that ELF radiation from VDTs may produce birth defects and miscarriages. We would like to see a large-scale epidemiological study of VDT operators and controls. We are asking NIOSH to do that, and I understand that this is under active consideration.

V. Future Directions
for
Industry, Labor and Public Policy

Let the Technology Adapt!

Elisabeth Reinhardt
POS Division
Apple Computer Inc.

This is a rare opportunity for me to have the chance to communicate to a "real" world, to people not part of the computer industry, about computers. As I was preparing for my topic with you today, I realized that I have had quite an involvement with ergonomics as it relates to computer technology. After growing up in Germany I came to school in the United States in the late 60's. There I was first confronted with computer technology. I remember noticing a friend's book that had "Fortran" written on it. I opened it, I looked at it, and didn't understand a word. That really frightened me, especially as I became aware that computer technology was popping up all over, running my bank account and my University account and so on.

I was to focus my remarks on that part of a computer system that makes it tick: *Software*—the lifeline of computers, if you will. Software is the area in which the quality of the human interface is largely decided. Probably 80 to 90% of the quality of a computer system is determined by the quality of the software.

Computer systems will not really be ergonomic unless the software inside them, that runs the tasks, is designed with ergonomics in mind. At this conference we have focused on important aspects of ergonomics, mostly aspects that can be measured in millimeters and inches, the way equipment can be moved about and positioned. But when you look at the impact of the system on the individual working with it, what is really important is the software. What software should do—especially the part of the software that determines how we interact—is to act as a bridge between the computer and the user. It seems to me that in many ways current software is like a bridge that does not quite span the river. It has gone only so far, and then we say: "You'll just have to swim to where the bridge starts." *The bridge must be built all the way to the users!*

When it comes to user interface design, the software available in the marketplace is lagging far behind what is technologically possible. It is very important to understand that. In 1973, James Martin wrote **Design of Man Machine Dialogue,** a landmark in the development of user research and user consciousness which looked at design issues from the point of view of serving users. Unfortunately, his insights have not become widely known or have not been considered by software designers.

John Couch, Vice President and general manager of the Personal Office Systems Division at Apple, tells that during the eight years he studied and taught computer science at the University of California at Berkeley he did not come across a single course in user interface design, not a single course. Good human interface design, or *ergonomic software*, is something we have just not paid a lot of attention. The industry is just beginning to realize how important it is to break down the barriers between the user and computer technology. We have been concentrating on getting ever more tasks performed ever faster and cheaper instead of determining whether faster and cheaper necessarily means that tasks are being performed better from the viewpoint of the user.

One reason, of course, is the price tag attached to really good, ergonomically designed, user interface software. It requires considerable investment of time, resources and commitment to user research on the part of the developing institution.

Probably the most important reason for the "underdeveloped" state of user interface software, however, is an underdeveloped consumer awareness. Lucy Suchman mentioned project RABBIT, a research project at Xerox PARC where the object is to improve the information retrieval situation. When someone doesn't quite know what they're looking for the system responds by offering limited information which gives the inquirer further ideas for the next question. If only such a service was available in the market place regarding ergonomic software! *Users and consumers do not know what they could be getting, so they don't know exactly what to ask for.*

Most of the systems introduced in recent years claim to be "user-friendly," that is *easy to use*. The question is: by whose standards are they user-friendly? Were the users asked? And if they were, did they really have enough information to make that assessment? How do you judge software quality? You can always say: "Yes, it's better than what I've used before." But do you know how good it could be? Most users do not know the difference between what they are currently using and what they could be getting.

A close look at that part of the software that determines the quality of the user interface shows that most systems make the user bend to it rather than bending to the needs of the user. Many of the user interfaces are hard to learn; in order to really utilize a package you have to acquire specialized knowledge. This situation is fine for some people, hobbyists and enthusiasts who thrive on it, or for those people who learn all the software packages that they can handle and then market themselves as specalists. But for the average person in the office who needs to get something done, it often represents a detour, a hindrance that has led many of them to say: "I don't want anything to do with computers."

It's time that these people finally get what they need and deserve. Let the technology adapt! Let's create ergonomic software with user interfaces that are shaped towards the people who use it.

To date one of the limiting factors in human interface design has been that the typical way to tell the computer what to do has been by using a formal language of commands which is entered character by character via a keyboard.

It's time to try a different approach, *graphics*, for instance. In many areas of information processing, graphics has already become a big success. In the charting of financial models, for example, where you compare this year's numbers with last year's, people understand the comparison at a glance when it is graphically outlined.

Can you imagine the effect of integrating graphics, i.e., pictures and symbols, into user interface? Can you imagine having a screen with symbols that would represent the different objects and functions? You are working with a particular document and decide that you want to see it printed. With a hand-operated pointing device you move the symbol representing your document over to the printer symbol. That's it! You don't have to type in a print command or the name of your document. The process is similar when you want to copy an important document from one diskette to another. After selecting "Duplicate" from the available function menu, there appears a duplicate image of your document from one diskette to another. After selecting "Duplicate" from the available function menu, there appears a duplicate image of your document on the screen which you then move over to the symbol representing your second disk drive. Simple, isn't it? The integration of graphics in conjunction with a pointing device (commonly referred to as a "mouse") provides a completely new intuitive means of interaction. I think that in a year or two we will be asking the question: "What is a computer without pictures?"

Another important feature of ergonomic software is a common user interface across all applications or, simply, *one way of doing things*. Let's say you have a word processor for your correspondence, a terminal for communicating with your big computer to handle data base queries and a personal computer to do budgeting and other kinds of analysis. How many computers are you going to put on your desk? How soon will you run out of space?

You want *one* computer that does all of these different tasks. Today there are more and more computers containing these functions on the market. But it is a serious problem that you have to learn a different way of interacting, a different set of commands, for each task. This is time consuming and increases the possibility of errors. Therefore, across all the different tasks that your computer is able to perform, you want one way to carry out equivalent functions.

Let's consider the screen on your CRT as a window. It's your window into the computer allowing you to see what's going on. If you want to do several things at one time you need several windows and they have to coexist on the screen. Only with that kind of flexibility can we approximate the way we work in the office.

Let's say you're working on your monthly report which includes a comparision of this month's results to last month's and you will also be consulting your latest PERT schedule for next month's objectives. You have at least three different sources to work from and you have them open side by side when the telephone rings. You can look up from your work, answer your telephone and then return to your report. You don't want to start again from scratch. Similarly, we want our computer to be able to keep track of various things side by side on one screen, at one time.

The final criterion in considering ergonomic software is possibly the most important one. You want to be able to mix and blend different kinds of information. This sounds pretty straightforward, but when you look at the necessary technology behind it you're talking about integrating textual information and graphic information. Quite a task! In today's office if you want all of these items blended together in your final report, you use scissors on the originals, cut and glue the parts together and rely on your copier to produce a completed picture. Thus the highest level of software integration would be to integrate different kinds of information and blend them together in one document so that at the time the document is printed the end product is exactly what you want.

In conclusion, let me summarize the key ingredients of ergonomic software. Firstly, the user interface is handled in a natural and consistent way across all applications eliminating the need to learn formal commands. What you will see in the coming year is the integration of graphics and information at the user level in order to communicate with the computer to get the job done. Secondly, you want the ability to work with several different applications on the screen simultaneously. And finally, you ultimately want cut-and-paste technology. You want to be able to blend information in just the way that you need it.

It shouldn't concern you whether this technology is difficult to develop. The user has the right to demand what is needed in the office.

Let me close with a quote. When Sir Isaac Newton was asked to explain how he came to make so many great discoveries, he said: "If I have been able to see farther than others, it is because I have stood on the shoulder of giants." Today, and in the last years in the software field, we have been standing on each other's feet!

Let the technology adapt. It can. It should. It will.

Building New Partnerships in a High-Tech Economy

Michael Dukakis
Governor of Massachusetts

It's a great pleasure to attend this conference, for it touches on something that will concern us more and more as time goes on. We are beginning in this country to try and anticipate what is going to happen to us as we move into an economy based increasingly on knowledge and on all the technology that goes with that. We are trying to deal with problems in a cooperative way before they become major problems in the first place.

We have a habit in this country of waiting until problems hit us between the eyes, and then wondering what happened. And we react with polarization and division and people arguing with each other and litigating against each other. But if we start early, and we bring people together—if we can bring the high technology industry together with the people who will be operating the machines that they produce—those of us in positions of political leadership can exercise that leadership more effectively and become coalition builders.

Those of you who have organized this first-ever event, and all of you who have taken the time to come and participate, are doing something very important for the future of this state and other states. All of you—office workers, company managers, and high tech manufacturers—

have come together to tackle the human side of the technological revolution.

And you have come together to ask three questions that truly are at the leading edge of economic policy.

How can we keep our knowledge-based economy growing, and creating the new jobs we need so badly?

How can we make sure that our people, and particularly working women, are equipped to take those jobs and build rewarding careers?

And how can we make sure that the quality of life in a rapidly-changing, technology-based workplace is safe, fulfilling, and fair?

It is very fitting that you have chosen Massachusetts to hold this conference. For the work you are doing, and the questions you are asking, have been shaped by the three great revolutions that were spawned in this Commonwealth.

It was the *American Revolution* that established the very principle that citizens can and must come together to solve the issues that affect our society.

It was the *Industrial Revolution*—born in this city, and in Lowell and Lawrence and Waltham and Brockton—that ushered in the economic miracles of decades past and the economic challenges of today. The labor movement itself—the assumption that workers can and should organize to improve their lives—sprang from the industrial cities and towns of this state.

And it is of course the *High Tech Revolution* that has shaped the questions you have come here together to address. Massachusetts was, and still is, the home of that revolution.

There is no denying that the economy of the future is an economy based on technology and knowledge. And that future is already here. In 1950 there were 12 computers in the United States. Today there are more than 600,000. The computer has transformed the way we live, and even more so the way we work. Half our workforce is employed in the "information sector" of our economy, and that proportion can only grow. If we want jobs for our people, and a healthy economic future, we simply must encourage that growth.

And make no mistake—the enemy of that growth is Reaganomics. Reaganomics is taking our economy apart job by job, and the problem is worse in our older industrial states. The human toll that this unworkable and uncaring economic philosophy is taking on working women and their families is devastating, and totally unacceptable. We need a more compassionate and more effective alternative—and this year's elections give all of us the chance to send that message to Washington, loud and clear.

And ironically, for an economic strategy that claims to favor the unfettered workings of the marketplace, Reaganomics has done precious little to help the high-tech growth industries grow. Their policies on education, on foreign trade, on research and development—all of these are hurting, not helping. One of the things I intend to do if I am elected Governor is to organize a High Tech Alliance with the governors of other technology states, so that we can do something about these policies as well.

Yet the creation of new jobs won't mean anything unless our people are prepared to work in them. And that means that in the next few years, this state and others must make it a top priority to prepare our workforce, still and always our greatest economic resource, to work effectively in an economy based increasingly on information technology.

I have proposed three ways to accomplish this goal in Massachusetts. First, our state's high-tech community and its colleges and universities, especially on the public side, have already begun to build a strong partnership around curriculum and research and development. More far-reaching proposals are being developed: for joint development of a microelectronics center; for joint training and funding of math and science teachers for our school system. I am committed to the support and nurturing of that partnership, and I know that many other people are around the country.

Second, I believe that every high school graduate in Massachusetts should know his or her way around a computer. And to make that happen, I have pledged to organize and lead a campaign for computer literacy in our public education system. The goal of this campaign is not to prepare every youngster for a career in high technology. But as everyone in this room understands, the workplace in general is coming to rely more and more on the innovations that technology provides.

To get a good job in a computer-operated machine shop, or a data processing room, or a cable TV system, or the modern business office itself, a young woman or man has to be computer-literate. How many of you in this audience could have had a better job sooner, or could be in a better position for career advancement, if information technologies had been a part of your basic high school education?

And third, every governor in America will have the opportunity, in fact a federal mandate, to rebuild his state's employment and training system from top to bottom starting in January 1983. The Congress has just passed, and the President has signed, pioneering legislation which, in substitution for the CETA system, will provide block grant money to the governors of the 50 states nearly $4 billion for employment and training. And it will be up to the governors, working with their businesses and citizens and their unions and labor organizations, all those who have a stake in jobs, to design employment and training and skill-building systems that fit the needs of that particular state.

For years we've been saying that government is obligated to retrain workers who've been left behind by a changing economy—to prepare them, while they're still young, for the jobs being created in our growth industries. For years we've been saying that government is obligated to see that women returning to the workforce have a shot at good jobs in careers with a future. Now we have the chance to do just that. In Massachusetts and many other states, government will have to bring together the best talents in business, labor, and education to make the pieces of an employment and training system mesh—so that people have every chance to cash in on the technological revolution.

Finally, you are here to set an agenda for quality of life in a technology-based workplace. You are here to get workers and managers talking now cooperatively and sensitively, about the steps that ensure occupational health and safety in an environment that is so very different from a construction site or a factory.

I have confidence in people, in their ability to solve problems if they get a little support and direction from government. I was Governor in the early days of OSHA, when worker health and safety often seemed to be at odds with the economic needs of business. I don't think it had to be that way, and I had my state Department of Labor and Industries provide free technical assistance to businesses trying to comply with OSHA requirements. And it worked. We helped companies do what needed to be done, while cutting through the tangle of red tape they feared. Our program had the support of business and labor alike.

Let me conclude by coming back to my main theme. We have had a tradition in this country of letting things happen and then beginning to pick up the pieces after damage has been done. It is very, very important that we not let that happen again. Yes this state was the home of the Industrial Revolution, and the Industrial Revolution at its best has meant a quality of life and standard of living for the people of the industrialized nations of the world that was unthinkable a century ago. But the Industrial Revolution brought with it very serious social and family and human consequences. It doesn't have to be that way. We know enough these days to anticipate problems and deal with them.

In closing I would like to applaud the coalition-building represented in this conference. We are going to do everything we can to work with you—to work with our high-tech companies, and with 9to5, and with all the organizations represented here. If we do that I believe that this state and other high-tech states can take advantage of growth, and jobs, and the best things that the knowledge revolution will bring us, without the kind of social and economic and human consequences that regretably we let happen during the Industrial Revolution.

Thank you for coming to Massachusetts and for inviting me to share my thoughts with you. To all of you, keep up the good work.

Experimental Approaches Towards Telecommunications in France

Hervé Nora
Director, Telematics Department
Ministère des P.T.T., France

I will present to you three of the main axes of the strategy of the French Telecommunications Administration:
- Electronic Mail Services;
- Videotext Services;
- Chip in the card or "Smart Card Systems;"

and show you the importance of, and the reasons for, the experimental approach we chose to use to develop these services.

These three components may not always relate directly to office work and office automation. First you must be aware of the fact that the evolution of white collar work in France follows a road different from that followed in the USA, or even in Germany and Sweden.

This difference may be explained by the fact that the growth of the information sector has not begun very long ago in French enterprises; also by the lack of awareness of the importance of office work for the productivity and efficiency of an entire enterprise. This may also be explained by the intense difficulties some enterprises encountered when they brought in computerization, which started later in France than in the USA, and which is still not achieved in many enterprises.

But the fact is that many enterprises: (1) are skeptical about the actual benefits of systematic office automation; (2) are skeptical about the actual capabilities of today's tools, are perplexed by the ever-growing range of equipment that manufacturers try to sell them; (3) think more in terms of new services to be offered to customers or new means of internal communication, rather than in terms of productivity gains through office automation; and (4) many enterprises are aware of and concerned about the impact of new technologies on their organization, or on the nature and interest of the tasks performed, and of the conditions under which they are performed.

A major consequence of these considerations is the frequent use of experimental approaches, and the search for external advisors, including the Telecommunications Administration which appears to have a leading role to play. This is related to our competence in some of the fields touched by office automation, as well as the recent development of the French telephone system. In addition, the good quality and adequacy to the needs of public data transmission network, Transpac, have restored our image in the country to consumers, and maybe magnified that image.

Another reason we are called upon to give advice is certainly because of our neutrality towards alternative technical trends and, of course, towards manufacturers. We do not manufacture any equipment, and voluntarily commercialize little equipment, especially no terminals besides our basic Videotext electronic directory system terminals, the $200 Minitext.

When we agree to play this role we have two main objectives: on the one hand, to sell phone calls and other telecommunications services; and on the other hand, to participate as a government agency in the development of the French economy. To achieve both these objectives, we have to carefully try to discover different needs, and to contribute to the development of new tools designed to match those needs, as well as to help our subscribers adequately use these tools. We see working with customers directly through experiments as the best way to accomplish these goals.

Electronic Mail Services

In the first field, that of electronic mail services, we began by becoming perfectly aware of what these terms meant, what they implied for the organization involved and for its employees. We consequently developed several experiments, one of which was the implementation of a country-wide network of word processors that communicated with one another. This experiment started in 1979. The network now includes more than 400 machines located in the secretary rooms of managers, and used by these secretaries. Their tools have changed, but not their jobs.

More than 800 women have volunteered to receive five days of specific training on the machines. They are assisted by monitors who come and see them regularly for a couple of months after the training. And a small centralized team is at their service to help them solve any problems they could have.

Today everybody considers that this operation was successful. The waiting list of volunteers is growing and cases of rejection are very rare. This experiment, and others that we conduct with enterprises in the field of facsimile systems, has led us to adopt a three-component strategy.

The first component is standardization. This is in order to avoid what has happened with data systems which very often are an obstacle to communication, rather than a tool of communication; and to increase the freedom of users to choose manufacturers. As you may know, facsimile devices are now rather well-standardized on an international basis, and the CCITT is working on the Teletext standards which should be achieved soon.

The second component of this strategy is the development of the basic tools. These tools include: new fax devices, such as the cheap ones that will be introduced on the French market at the beginning of next year; standardized Teletext machines, the cheap ones being available in 1983; and private store-and-forward message switching systems for both fax and Teletext systems.

The third component of our strategy is of course concerned with public networks: we are pursuing the development of Transpac, the public data network, and of its interconnections with the other networks.

We are very rapidly digitalizing the phone network while our digital domestic satellite system, Telecom 1, will be launched by the end of 1983.

We finally are developing the interconnection between Telex and Teletext in order to widen the possibilities of the Telex devices, as well as to give the opportunity to the first Teletext owners to call all over the world the one million enterprises that are equipped with Telex. This interconnection should be available in 1984.

Videotext Services

The second axis of our strategy I would like to present to you is the development of Teletel, the French Videotext System.

International standardization committees are fond of barbarian terms. The word "Videotext" covers a combination of TV screen and phone line access to any kind of computer services using specific standards. Initially, Videotext was conceived of in order to offer domestic data retrieval services through the home television set. Everywhere in the world experiments were conducted, such as the Dusseldorf and Berlin trials in Germany, and the Velizy trial in France. In France, however, three facts combined to lead to a rather different policy.

First was an ergonomic consideration. The use of a typewriter keyboard rather than a purely digital one enabled us to avoid the unaccepted true research system, and to use much more intelligent software, as well as to offer such services as domestic electronic mail services. (This was one of the greatest successes, an unforecasted one, of the Velizy experiment.) Services also included educational programs and electronic directory services.

The second consideration was philosophical: we definitely adopted a totally decentralized approach for our Videotext system, letting service providers choose their computer premises and their software. The consequences were a second widening of the range of services, and the emergence of microsystems used by companies that wanted to offer very precise services, and even by individuals.

The third fact was the decision itself to launch the electronic directory service, which led to the development of very cheap Teletel terminals, which are presently rented at $10 a month, maintenance included, in the areas where the electronic directory service is not offered, or to the enterprises who want a greater number of terminals in the areas where the service is offered.

These three facts have combined to induce a strong demand for the professional use of Teletel terminals and networks in quite every sector of the economy: mail order companies as well as supermarkets, banks as well as insurance companies, physicians as well as farmers, newspapers as well as in administration.

The objectives always are to implement application and services for which traditional data transmission and processing systems appear irrelevant, whether because of their cost or because of their complexity to use, or most often both. These applications generally deal with better services offered to customers, retailers, sub-contractors and so on. And quite often they involve occasional users, those people who use them once or twice a day, to once or twice a month.

In every case has the experimental approach been followed. More than 40 experiments are presently conducted all over France with more than 5,000 terminals. Some have already been positive, and the decision to make them widespread has been taken. Although I do not know which ones, some will certainly lead to negative decisions. Today our forecast is that besides the development of the electronic directory service (which is estimated to be 200,000 terminals in 1983, 600,000 to 800,000 in 1984, and 2 million by the end of 1985) a wide market is opening for the professional use of Teletel—20,000 terminals by the beginning of 1983, and between 150,000 and 300,000 by the end of 1984.

Experimenting with the "Smart Card"

The third and last axis which I think is of interest today is the chip in the card or "Smart Card" program. Take a classical magnetic stripe plastic card, introduce a microprocessor and memory into it, plus the adequate software, and you get a powerful, secure and confidential new tool able to solve numerous problems—of payment, identification, data collection, storage and data retrieval. This card can guarantee privacy and be used for several purposes by several different entities.

Here again, the experimental approach is systematically followed by the Telecommunications Administration as well as by enterprises. We experiment with the use of "Smart Cards" for the payment of Teletel services and of telephone calls in public phones; banks are presently experimenting with the cards in POS terminals (250,000 card holders) and for home banking services; while the Department of Health will by the middle of next year be experimenting with it to replace the illness paper sheet used by the Social Security system. Cable TV organizations also will try this to solve payment problems.

What are our tentative conclusions? In France, the experimental approach is pursued both for technical and economical reasons, and because of our awareness of the importance of the organizational and social effects of technology. This is not because every manager of every organization has added social or human objectives to their traditional ones, but because even those who have not still realize the strong interrelations between the three challenges they confront with the development of office automation: productivity, working conditions, and task enrichment.

As for myself, I am convinced that technology is neutral. Because of telecommunications, technically centralized systems can be used for decentralized applications, while decentralized systems (the main trend of the future) can be used for centralization. These kinds of systems may or may not contribute to task enrichment or improved working conditions.

First and foremost, it is a question of the general policy of the enterprise or organization involved. After this first condition is fulfilled, it is then mainly a question of correctly assessing the immediate and future consequences of the choices that are made.

Women and the Fight Around Office Automation

Madame Cecile Goldet
Parliament of France

I am a politician, and until last April, I have also been a gynecologist and psychologist for 40 years. I lived with the difficulties and occurences of thousands of women, and have seen the effect of their way of life on their mental and physical health. For this reason I felt obliged to try and contribute to changing society, through political activity, to help modify and improve women's lives.

Over the past five, six, seven years, I have seen a new pathology appear among my patients, and I began to become interested in these computers, whose effects were so disturbing to the people who had to face them at work.

In fact, I do not know if this new pathology I have seen was due to this new sort of work, or to the changing of work. It is really difficult for a woman who has been a typist for 15 years to begin working on a computer. They often fear that they will not be able to cope with it, and stay in fear of losing their jobs. This mental constraint, I suppose, is part of their difficulties. But it is truly impossible today to say for sure if it is the computer that had the effect on the health of the person who uses it. So I don't want to say anything about that. The studies that are going on are very important.

Permanent Vigilance

As you see, I am not a specialist. I came here hoping to learn a lot from our different experiences. And I have learned a lot. Information processing and office automation is not the first technological revolution. It is not the first time that workers stay in awe of technological progress, fearing it will act to suppress their jobs. In France, as in England and other countries, workers once tried to destroy the new textile machines which they thought would take away their jobs. In fact, the new technology gave them an entirely different possibility of working at better jobs for better wages.

But this technological revolution appears in a totally different context. First, we have a good deal of information about it, and through it will have more access to all kinds of information. We can decide to act, and we must act. We can try to master the new technology, rather than be completely dominated by it as we were 100 years ago.

But it is a problem to imagine, even partly, what alternative office technology would look like. Was it possible in 1880 to imagine 1980 factories, or in 1960 to imagine microprocessors? Neither is it possible to imagine the computers of 1999. Things are changing, and will go on changing more and more rapidly. We must stay permanently vigilant and active about what is going on or happening.

The Struggle of Women and Unions

Mobilization of the unions concerning the risks and difficulties of the new computers has come late, and has not been enough, mainly because the computers first invaded offices where mostly women are working. And there are not many women in the unions. Most of them work in their offices and their homes full time, and they have no time to be active in the unions. Most of them are not ready to fight. And we all know that men are not especially interested in that sort of problem so long as they consider them to be specifically feminine. This is why the struggle of '9to5' is so important—to put the question of women's role in its proper place.

In fact, the consequences of computers on employment are not very well known. It is certain that a number of jobs will be suppressed here, and that a great number of jobs will be created somewhere else. But which jobs? How many of them? And who will be concerned? We don't know yet.

We must fight so that no worker is put out of a job because of computers, and that each worker be given a fair chance at a decent job, even if it is not the same job. Professional training is important, for it gives workers the possibility of using these new gadgets with the least detrimental consequences to their nervous and physical health. (Training should open to the workers a wide range of possibilities to enrich their jobs.) But is has not been sufficiently studied how to best use these possibilities.

It is not enough to give the user a utilization manual and just hope that the user will become fully acquainted with the computer. There needs to be a more extensive training period so that the worker becomes familiar not only with a single computer, but with the kinds of computers that may come in the future. This sort of long training is generally not offered. And when the training is not enough, naturally the supplementary effects of fatigue and loss of time and energy will affect the users.

The Role of Legislation

In France, where the process of informatization is less advanced than in the States or in Sweden, we are aware of these problems and we hope to introduce computers while at the same time fighting so that we have the minimum risks for users, and be sure that no one will lose his job. If one desires this result, it is essential that action be taken as soon as possible when office automation is decided, or even before, when it is being considered. If we don't obtain the advice and input of workers before they have to sit down in front of the computer, nothing can be done. It is then necessary that the unions consider this a major item. And it is utterly necessary that women enter the fight with all their forces.

What does it mean the President Francois Mitterrand has chosen to give the computer industry a big, a major, chance? At the same time, the unions, women's organizations and especially our Ministry of Women's Rights are actively studying all aspects of the dangers, the risks, and the difficulties of computers. We aim to try and prevent the bad aspects rather than having to cure them.

Some people here have spoken of the necessity of legislation to prevent the possible dangers of computers. I don't think this is the right way to go at the process. Law may intervene only after the struggle by the workers themselves, after their own experiences have pointed to the decisions that must be made. Afterwards, when these results have been obtained, law must intervene so that the results of these battles and victories can be extended to all users.

The place of the unions in this stuggle is essential, and must stay essential. The unions must remain a force of opposition, and a promoter of discussion, whatever the government is. I think that the first struggle is on the working ground, not on the legalistic one. For it is each of us who has to fight for all the others.

Alternative Models of Worker Participation

Leslie Schneider
John F. Kennedy School of Government
Harvard University

If there has been any single theme to emerge from this conference, it is, perhaps, that technological change and the direction it takes is a matter of social choice. There are no simple or direct causal relationships between specific technological changes and various social consequences, be they positive or negative. Some of the speakers have argued that while technology may set certain limits to the way we organize work, there are still many choices to be made about the development, implementation, and use of new technologies. Both managers and workers as individuals and through their unions influence these decisions, either informally or formally. It is also important to realize that workers' demands have already begun to shape the direction of office automation.

A number of European speakers over the past two days have talked about their efforts to set certain standards for the design of VDTs. In effect, they have forced vendors in both Europe and America to design better machines. American workers have benefitted from these efforts.

What's more, more and more managers are talking about the ideas that we have discussed these past few days—worker participation, work redesign, social and organizational consequences. In fact, one professor of management at the Sloan School at MIT, Peter Keen, even goes so far as to call office automation a "highly political process."

This may sound good, but our work has barely begun. Because even though more and more managers are using terms like ergonomics, or work redesign and worker participation, the key task is to give these ideas precise content, to determine what they actually mean for office workers. Put another way: participation is important, but to what end, or more specifically, for whose ends? That's what I'll talk about in this paper.

The Least They Can Do

Let me quickly review three examples of office automation that illustrate the spectrum of approaches to participation and work redesign, with a special emphasis on this question of "to what end" and "for whom."

First, let me issue a word of warning about vendors and their new-found emphasis on properly designed equipment. "Ergonomics" is the buzz-word, said a marketing representative at Wang. Certainly it's very important that more and more word processors are being designed according to comprehensive health and safety standards. But we have to realize that this won't necessarily solve all the social, organizational, or managerial problems. If you sit all day and type at a Wang word processor, you don't necessarily have a more interesting or meaningful job than if you sit all day and type at a Lexitron or Xerox word processor.

We should think of well-designed equipment as something like the minimum wage: it's the very least they can do!

Let's move on to a much more detailed example of new technology and work redesign, one that's received a great deal of publicity and been written up in the **Harvard Business Review**. That is CitiBank's program to automate its "back office" processing services in New York City. The Paradise Project, as management calls it, is supposed to be the epitome of successful technological change and work redesign. First, managers redesigned the work of the clericals so that their jobs would be more integrated and have greater potential for professional advancement. Then, they brought in a new computer technology to support these newly redesigned jobs. Employees participated in some phases, particularly in designing the work environment, testing office chairs, and picking color schemes.

The result, says CitiBank, was a situation in which both productivity and the quality of service improved, as well as satisfaction of workers and customers. The only problem, I would say, is that the participatory process at CitiBank was totally conceived and carried out by the managers. It was they who determined what the new jobs would be, and they who picked the employees who would be trained for them. As a result, while CitiBank's work-station professionals seem happier with their new jobs now, these jobs have aspects that I think few of us would consider appropriate for a professional's work environment. For example, CitiBank's back office employees are monitored by computers which print out detailed records of their work performance daily. It will be interesting, I think, to see how these people feel about their jobs in five years time.

A Highly Political Process

But there have also been cases of office automation where employee participation has been much more elaborate and serious than the efforts at CitiBank, even in the United States. In a small department of a large bank located in the U.S., for example, an office automation task force was formed to study the possibilities of using office automation to solve the problems of work load and poor working conditions. The task force included both professional employees and support staff. For one year they had meetings every week and studied not only the available technological options, but also alternative ways to organize the work. They developed a very well-thought-out and detailed plan that they were going to present to their management. There was only one problem: the bank's office technology department, which buys the equipment, found out about this and tried to veto it.

The workers in this particular department were lucky. They had a sympathetic administrator who pushed the plan through. But if this hadn't happened, the group (neither the managers nor the secretaries) wouldn't have had the power to do anything about it. What eventually happened is that the technical recommendations of the proposal were implemented, but those concerning the reorganization of work have been put on the back burner. To this day, they have still not been acted on.

Finally, I'd like to conclude with a case study from Norway as an illustration of how the same principles we've heard about at this conference—work reorganization, worker participation—look in a very different social and political context. Both Kari Thoresen and Lisbet Hjort discussed this social context earlier in the conference. Now let's look at what this means in a specific situation: a program to engage workers in the automation of a teller system at a Norwegian bank.

What began as a technological change project turned into a campaign to totally re-organize work at the bank. Unlike workers at CitiBank, the clericals at this bank were involved in actually designing the new technological system, planning its implementation, and redesigning the jobs. A group composed almost entirely of tellers designed and debugged the technical system, and a union management group investigated its social and organizational consequences.

The real problem, they found, was not so much the technology itself, but, to quote from their final report, "how the work and authority structure are organized." Unlike the workers in the last bank example, these workers had the power to actually turn their recommendations into reality. They have begun to make substantial organizational changes in the way work is done at the bank. They have even redesigned the job of the president—at his request, I might add.

In short, given a context where unions and workers have both established structures for genuine participation, and have the power to carry through their proposals, technological change can truly become a "highly political process," one that works to the benefit of clerical workers—although perhaps not in the way that managers from the Sloan School would be completely comfortable with.

What kind of guidelines can we draw from these examples? What kind of principles are relevant for office workers facing new technology? The first lesson might be, if you have a union in your office, use it to get a handle on these issues. And if you don't have a union, form one. But in the meantime, watch out for wolves in sheeps' clothing, for short-term management-initiated efforts that offer neither genuine opportunities for participation, nor the power to carry them through. Instead, we have to begin now to start figuring out what we want to get out of the new technology, how we want to use it, what kind of jobs we want to support.

And finally, we have to begin to take the first steps toward creating structures at our workplaces so that we can begin to control technology on our own terms. Otherwise, things will go on as they do now. Someone else will decide for us.

Collective Bargaining Strategies on New Technology:
The Experience of West German Trade Unions

Regine Meyer
Division for White Collar Workers
IG Metall, Federal Republic of Germany

I would like to give you a report on alternative approaches to the use of new technologies by the West German trade unions. Although I cannot speak for all of the 17 unions united in the German Trade Union Federation, the DGB, I will give you a brief survey of the main resolutions concerning new technologies enacted by the last DGB Congress in May 1982. These resolutions have been agreed upon by all member unions.

Detailed information, especially insofar as practical experiences and results are concerned, I can only give you for my union, the German Metal Workers union, IG Metall, which is the largest in the DGB with a total of 2.6 million members. About 378,000 of these are white collar workers.

Unfulfilled Promise of Office Automation

First let me give you an overview of the social experiences and conflicts that constitute the background to union demands relating to new technologies. Our programs and strategies do not result from theoretical formulations, but rather from painful negative experiences with rationalization in the past. We now are estimating the main impact of new technologies on job security and working conditions still to come in the late 1980s.

The most alarming effect of new technologies is, of course, the loss of jobs. Registered unemployment of white collar workers in West Germany presently amounts to more than 600,000; this number would be increased by another one-third or one-half if unregistered jobless, mostly women and youths, were added in. Between 60 and 70% of the registered unemployed non-manual workers are female. A number of factors—Taylorism, low qualification requirements, and traditional women's roles, among others—made it rather simple for employers to automate female jobs first. Meanwhile, we are now reaching the crucial point where male non-manual workers are also largely affected by rationalization strategies.

Undoubtedly, the current worldwide business recession has a great impact on the labor market and unemployment levels. But recession and automation are closely linked, for employers use new technologies as one way of decreasing costs in the hope of surviving a recessionary period.

Lowering costs, however, also means shrinking purchasing power while productivity and output are constantly rising. Or to put this into a simple slogan: Too few people are working too much.

But not only the number of jobs is diminishing, but the quality of working conditions of those still employed in many cases is worsening, too, as a result of the application of new technologies. Preceding the introduction of computer systems, the work usually is fragmented, simplified and standardized, leading to a downgrading of qualification, responsibility and payment. Under these circumstances working with computers means working more intensively, more rapidly, and under minute control.

Of course, the introduction of computers means certain improvements on the workers' side, as for instance speeding up information-retrieval processes or being released from troublesome routine work, but these are only accidental by-products of automation, never the main goal. Within the framework of a capitalist economy, automation and new technologies are primarily introduced in order to lower costs, to eliminate jobs, to downgrade payments, and to obtain an almost perfect supervision of workers.

Nevertheless, we do not reject new technologies altogether knowing that they could be used in order to really improve and facilitate working conditions. In our opinion the negative effects are not necessary consequences of new technologies, but the result of their exclusively capital-orientated utilization. For us the crucial question is: Whose interests do they serve?

Office automation does not necessarily have to follow the patterns it is presently given by employers and profit-orientated consultants. It does not necessarily have to result in unemployment, degrading of qualification and payments, Taylorism, health damage and supervision. New technologies could lead to still-unheard-of flexibility in work organization.

At the same time, the enormous increase in productivity that automation makes possible could also provide the necessary financial resources to create a real humanization of working conditions in terms of improving skills, working environment, payment conditions; decreasing stress and health damage; and allowing additional breaks and the shortening of working hours. This would be a rational application of the immense possibilities offered by new technologies.

Our union proposals are characterized by the principle of not rejecting new technologies altogether, but putting them to the service of workers. Of course there are certain uses of computer technology that we refuse right away, such as the computer-aided surveillance systems which even now exceed the most horrible science fiction imaginations like Huxley's **Brave New World** or Orwell's **1984**. But on the whole we do see the possibilities to influence the introduction of office technologies according to our proposals.

Such influence, of course, is not realized automatically. Quite the contrary. Employers have strictly rejected our demands for co-determination in the application of new technology and shortening of working hours in a so-called "declaration of taboos," so we are facing severe social conflicts. The employer's discretionary power over capital (that is over investments, jobs and working conditions) has to be limited if there is to be any progress on the labor side. Private profit strategies of rationalization in combination with supply-side economics of governments have sufficiently proven incapable of solving the present problems of economic and social crisis.

Millions of workers are suffering from unemployment, social insecurity and growing poverty. We have to put an end to this sort of crisis-management which makes the poor pay the bill of the rich.

Basic Union Demands

Now, what are conceivable and realistic alternatives to look like? Of course there is no simple answer, or a one-and-only solution, on the part of the unions. A set of problems as manifold and complicated as office automation (and workshop automation as well) cannot be approached except by a combination of strategies, by different means and on different levels.

The first level and the focus of any operation is the job in the office. Work has to become dignified and designed according to the needs and wants of human beings, instead of adapting men to most imperfect and in many cases just humiliating working conditions. New technology and work organization, the results of human intelligence and skill, finally have to be put into the service of working people themselves.

Therefore West German unions almost unanimously make the following claims as far as the introduction of new technology on a company level is concerned.

• Human and social requirements have to be prior, or at least equal to, economic considerations.

• Maintaining if not upgrading the social standard in terms of payment, skills and responsibility.

• No dismissals due to the introduction of new technology; workers forced out of a job on account of rationalization have to be offered new jobs equivalent with regard to payment and qualification.

• The design of office equipment and environments (for instance, furniture, machines, Video Display Terminals, climate, lighting, etc.) have to suit human needs.

- Health protection by periodical medical consultation during working hours; additional paid-for breaks for VDT typists of 10 minutes per hour; limitation of VDT-working to half of the daily working hours, at the maximum. By these demands we hope to encourage managers to assign a variety of tasks to office staff in order to prevent occupational stress, visual fatigue and muscle strain.
- Agreements on the amount of work to be accomplished in a certain period, which up to now hasn't been typical for office work.
- Limitations on the kind, the number and the purpose of personal data collection by computer systems, in order to prevent a total surveillance of the staff and the misuse of data.
- Safeguarding, respectively, the implementation of a work organization that provides for interesting, diversified jobs granting for skilled and responsible work. We are calling for a design of computer systems which enables clerical workers to achieve competent use of computers as a tool, instead of being reduced to the role of a subordinate data collector. The principles of job enrichment and job rotation have to be introduced in office work in order to avoid monotonous, inferior, sickness-causing jobs.

The last problem is the most difficult to resolve: changing work organization according to human needs is obviously interfering with employers' preogatives. There are, however, difficulties, too, on the part of union representatives and the personnel involved. Presenting proposals concerning work organization means intervening in a field traditionally left over to the employer. Furthermore, implementation of diversified skilled jobs requires a high amount of interest, engagement, additional training, flexibility and so forth on the side of the employees.

It's not an easy task to redesign a pool of unskilled data entry typists into a versatile office team doing a broad variety of different jobs. We also found it quite difficult to find programmers familiar with the needs of intelligent, responsible computer work.

In most cases programming is done far away from the actual users. Programmers usually are aiming at a maximum "elegance" and error-security of programs, which on the side of office personnel may turn out as highly monotonous, fragmented, tedious work. Thus we urgently need research on human-like program design and a close cooperation between programmers and users. The creation of improved, skilled office work calls for more than exterior changes like VDT design, illumination or even decentralization. The whole program outline has to be altered if computer-systems are to be at the service of working people. Up to now management strategies are aimed at submitting people to machines. Not only have the tasks to be varied and enriched, but working procedures must be improved according to increasing responsibility and job satisfaction.

Nevertheless, we have to pursue our proposals if we want to change from the role of reacting and repairing damages to the part of active influence and preventing damages.

Union Counter-Action Strategies

As you will have guessed, there are only few positive examples of this sort of aggressive counter-action. Yet such examples do exist, and have proven that new technology can be applied in a completely different way. Let me briefly outline one positive experience in the reorganization of the clerical service in a northern German town administration. Here new technology, electronic typewriters and word processors, were introduced in a long-term cooperative process between the secretaries and typists involved, and executives and union representatives.

In this case study, the employees and employers and union not only co-determinated in choosing the machines and office equipment, but also worked out a new model of office organization. Secretaries and typists went through different training courses in order to get an overview of the whole administrative process, as well as to learn how to control the new machines competently. The working hours saved by using machines were left to the women, in order to participate in activities formerly done by executives. So there were no dismissals but a training and upgrading of the women workers. The executives set up a list of activities coming into question for a turnover to the women, and the women had the chance to choose and make changes after a certain period of experience. As a result there are office teams able to meet a variety of different demands with more competence, more interest and more satisfaction in work.

Undoubtedly this is only a model which cannot be simply transferred to any private company administration, but it gives us the opportunity to show that new technology can be implemented as an extension for the employee within a process of skilling personnel. Above all, it proves that office staff is willing to cooperate in a complicated training and decision process.

As to the other items on the above list of demands, a considerable number of company agreements of different quality have been achieved. The poorest ones only refer to the outward design of furniture, VDTs, etc.; the better ones also provide for additional breaks of 5 to 10 minutes per hour, a daily limit on VDT-working, agreements against misuse of data, job security stipulations, etc.

The job security effect of these agreements is limited, though, in that only the present personnel is protected. In many companies the number of jobs is permanently declining by attrition. A problem happens with regard to payment guarantees: the present employee is protected but the newcomer, if there is any, is downgraded. On the whole, we are not able to cope with mass unemployment on the company level and by means of agreements based upon the Works Constitution Act.

The second level of union counter-action consists of collective bargaining. Certainly an active pay policy still is on top of our claim list. Nevertheless, maintaining social security and improving job quality are of equal importance. Reductions of unemployment are inconceivable without a considerable shortening of working hours, income compensation granted.

I may add that West German unions unanimously are opposed to a spread of part time work, job sharing, computer work at home, etc., because reduction of working hours without income compensation means further decrease of purchasing power and undermines our struggle for a 35-hour week. Furthermore, the increase of part time work under the present circumstances tends to create a flexible reserve of underprivileged personnel, especially of women and youths.

Thus the Congress of the German Trade Union Federation in May '82 agreed upon a coordinated strategy between the member unions in order to obtain the 35-hour week, income compensation provided. Steps on this way may be special regulations for certain groups like elderly workers or shift-working employees. Different forms of work-time reduction being considered include shortening of worklife, that is, early retirement; shortening of the worktime per year, that is more vacations: and shortening of the weekly working hours and additional paid-for breaks during the working day.

The executive of my organization just decided to emphasize the weekly reductions and to demand the 35-hour week, as soon as the contract on working time comes up for renewal at the end of 1983.

On the level of collective bargaining, the reduction of working time is the most important but not the only countermeasure regarding rationalization. We are also demanding procedures of information and co-determination exceeding the law with respect to the introduction of new technology. Sufficient information at an early planning stage is of vital importance to the works councils and union representatives if they want to do more than minor modifications of given facts.

Another important problem is the humanization of working conditions and new modes of payment scales and job descriptions. Presently payments depend on the skill actually called for at a given job. If the employer decreases the need of skill by organizational changes or by use of new technology, the payments, too, can be downgraded. This is not only a theoretical possibility but a painful experience of thousands of workers. Therefore, we are calling for income guarantees regardless of changes in the skill requirements of jobs. Thus the incentive to fragment and deskill work constantly in order to save labor costs would be taken from the employers.

It would be overestimating collective bargaining, if we pretended that it could solve all problems subsequent to automation on the one hand, and to supply-side economics on the other, by industrial agreements. Even if we succeeded in an immediate reduction of working time to 35 hours weekly it would not be sufficient to compensate for unemployment.

Promoting Qualitative Economic Growth

A realistic strategy to conquer the economic crisis has to combine comprehensive measures of shortening worktime with a medium-term government policy aiming at what we call qualitative growth. By this we mean planned efforts to cover needs in deficient sectors such as social security, education, housing, urban transport, energy saving, environmental protection, etc. Labor-oriented research and development policy, especially regarding the use of new technology, also fits into this conception.

Furthermore German trade unions are calling for a fundamental reform of the system of social security, the field of medical care, occupational health prevention, etc., as well as regarding pension funds.

You might, however, be interested in the special measures concerning VDTs already taken by the trade supervisory authorities. The hazards posed to the clerical workers by VDTs have initiated an intensive debate in the unions as well as in public opinion. In fact there has never been so much concern about a new technology before.

Thus within a few years regulations for the protection of VDT-typists were set up. Even though they do not satisfy our claims this is a basis for further legislation. At least we now have minimum standards for job design as to the VDT, furniture, illumination, climate, space, etc. Periodical eye-check-ups are part of the regulations, too. Additional breaks and versatility of job content are recommended.

The German Trade Union Federation has presented detailed proposals how to master the economic recession, create new jobs and maintain public welfare. We not only set up claims but also made valid suggestions as to the fundraising. I will not go into details, but let me just mention two facts of vital importance:

First of all, unemployment doesn't save any money if you thoroughly analyze it. Presently the cost of unemployment in West Germany including the shortfall of the gross national product amounts to about 150 billion DMK a year. A significant part of an employment program would therefore be "self-financing."

Secondly, job security also has to be put under the heading of peace and disarmament strategies. As we all know the arms race eats up the money we desperately need to create new jobs and to defend the welfare state. It is worth bearing in mind that, according to US calculations, a billion dollars invested in the defense industry only results in 75,000 jobs whereas in the construction industry it equals 100,000 jobs, in public health 139,000, and in the field of education even 187,000 jobs would come out. In fact, the defense industry is one of the front runners in rationalization and job elimination. Shifting budgetary funds from the military to the service industries would at the same time make our world safer and meet the necessities of occupational and social security.

Reason and humanism are on our side. Our proposals are realistic and substantiated. Yet they will meet rigid resistance from the employers and their political protectors. It will take us enormous efforts to push our claims through, especially since office staff is rather poorly unionized at this time.

All the more that I am pleased by having the opportunity to participate in this conference. International exchange of information and developing coordinated union strategies is urgently needed. "Multinational and financial corporations are leading the race towards the office of the future in the belief that office automation will guarantee them spiralling profits," states 9to5 in its analysis. That's right. And they are playing the game on an international level. They are playing off one national union against the other. Computer technologies offer to them more and more possibilities of worldwide supervision and competition between personnel, of shifting jobs from one country to the other, thereby undermining grievances and strikes. If we are going to win the race we have to speed up our international activities considerably.

Taking the Initiative on New Technology:

Canadian Labor Approaches

Fred Pomeroy
Canadian Labour Congress
Standing Committee on Microelectronics

I would like to bring you up to date on what the Standing Committee on Microelectronics of the Canadian Labour Congress is all about. So I will be talking about the overall game plan rather than specific issues. In Canada we often think that we are not doing enough about new technology, but in fact there is too much going on for me to be able to tell you about everything. So I will adopt a rather broad-brush approach.

What are we doing in our committee in Canada? There has been a lot of talk about issues at this conference, but little discussion about how you go out about implementing our responses to those issues. Perhaps I'll be able to add something on that.

Among my own union, the Communications Workers of Canada, and other unions, we first started dealing with technological change in Canada in a formal way back in the middle of 1979. We set up a telecommunications council, made up of a number of unions, and its purpose was to deal with a government review that was taking place on telecommunications policy. We soon realized, however, that the focus of that council and its make-up, only telecommunications unions, was far too narrow. It was quite apparent that the information revolution and converging technologies were having an impact on everyone in all sectors of the economy, not just in telecommunications.

So it was exactly the kind of problems and factors discussed at this conference that caused us to set up our committee. We regarded those issues as being so serious that we set up a standing committee on technology in mid-1981. Every union affiliated to the Canadian Labour Congress was asked to participate, and we were happy to see an overwhelming response by the unions to committee activities.

A Three-Pronged Approach

Roughly stated, the committee has three different purposes. First, to enable us to get a grip on what's taking place; to get an overview of the technology that's coming in, and get we union people up to speed on the various piece-parts of the technology.

Secondly, we are attempting to sort out what the issues are that we are going to have to deal with. And thirdly, the committee's job is to sort out appropriate responses which will give us a position where we will be able to take the initiative on the introduction of new technology—rather than being locked into our traditional position of just reacting to technological change after it comes into place.

At the very outset we rejected taking a Luddite position. We felt that new technology can be used to improve our lives by eliminating dangerous, repetitive, boring work; to create new services, such as medical procedures which are very much needed by our society; and it can be used to give us more free time to pursue our other interests away from what has traditionally been considered as work. In our view, it's not a question of whether or not there should be new technology. It's a very serious question about how it will be used and for whom. Ultimately, as Helga Cammell of FIET has pointed out, it's a question of power, and that is the ultimate issue our committee is coping with.

There is no divine law, nor is there any technical requirement, that some people in our society have to make a sacrifice in order that others might make social progress through the introduction of new technology. That's a human decision, and it's the way things will be run unless we, who are impacted by new technology, take action to make sure that decisions are made in our interests. To make sure that happens, our committee has subdivided itself into three subcommittees: on collective bargaining, on legislation, and on education. Let me talk for a bit about the activities they have been carrying out.

Like many of the trade unions in Europe, we see the legislative process as particularly important. Employees have to be organized before they can effectively bargain collectively, and there are a number of impediments to getting organized in Canada. Secondly, there are certain issues such as retraining and health and safety standards that require remedies wider than you can effectively deal with in collective bargaining. Thirdly, runaway employers are impossible to bargain with. If they take off to the third world, it's hard for us in Canada to negotiate a collective agreement.

Probably the most reason for legislative action is that we need a commitment to full employment at the government level. As long as no such commitment exists, and there's a de-skilling of work and a large pool of unemployed, employers are going to be in the driver's seat. Consequently, our legislative subcommittee has been developing programs that we are pursuing with various levels of government in Canada.

But we don't just believe in dealing with the issues of technology in the legislative forum. We're putting a very high priority on collective bargaining. Our collective bargaining subcommittee has been developing a handbook for collective bargaining to provide unions with background data, and serve as a ready reference source to determine what has been achieved in other areas. The manual will be out soon, and one of its authors, Jane Stinson of the Canadian Union of Public Employees, is attending this conference.

Building Greater Awareness

It has become quite clear to us that, unfortunately, in Canada, everyone in the labor movement is not at the same level of awareness about these issues, about the pace of the introduction of new technology and the magnitude of technological change. And that goes all the way to the top officers in a number of unions. We found some people who have been lulled to sleep by past events, when technology was introduced on a piece-meal basis and more highly-skilled people were required at the end of the process. Some early computer applications provide examples of this.

In other cases we've found that leaders and members at different levels of union organizations are distracted by the economic crisis, seeing that as the only priority. They don't see the fine hand of technological change as a key player in the whole mess.

Consequently, our education subcommittee is embarking on a major program to get the whole labor movement, at all levels, up to speed on these issues, hopefully by next summer. This is a rather ambitious program to undertake in a country as diverse as Canada. Our goal is to get everyone to understand that technological change is not just an issue that will become less meaningful and eventually go away. It is a fundamental part of the economic crisis, and will serve to sustain the economic crisis and the unemployment that we will endure in the future—unless we come to some collective decisions and take some action to come to grips with it. We are doing this in several different ways.

One set are called "awareness courses." These will be made available to leaders and members across the country at all levels of union organizations to bring them up to speed with the issues and what has to be done. Another area we are working on is "skills courses" to help train the staff and leaders who will be involved in collective bargaining, to make them more effective at dealing with those issues.

Improvements in Working Conditions

So we are working very hard in Canada to influence the shape of the future. We also have been racking up a number of successes or improvements along the way, both in the public and the private sectors. One of the most important, though it tends to be unnoticed and understated, is the heightened profile that technological change has gained in Canada in the last couple of years. There has been a tremendous change in the reaction of people and in the numbers that know what's going on with technology and are actively working to find solutions.

Probably the best known gain that we have been able to achieve in Canada has been a series of agreements to move pregnant women away from working with VDTs. More and more unions have been gaining such agreements in Canada. I personally see this as a rather limited option, because we are rapidly approaching a situation in which more and more jobs involve VDT technology. As you reach that point, there are less and less options for work to place pregnant women in. We need a longer-term program: either get rid of VDTs or make them safe to work with.

In the meantime we are working to make them safer to deal with. A number of unions in Canada have negotiated for VDT operators more frequent and longer rest breaks. The pace of these contracts is quickening. A number of agreements in Canada now provide for retraining for other jobs when technological change creates redundancies. However, most of these entail retraining programs within the same employers' environment as the technology is being introduced, and very often they do not include a guarantee of the same rate of pay or work location. We need a broader program in this area as well.

I appreciate the opportunity to explain a number of things that we are doing, and I hope that you have a better understanding of developments on these issues in Canada.

Legislative and Research Options for the U.S. Congress

Dennis Houlihan
Labor Standards Subcommittee
Committee on Education and Labor
U.S. House of Representatives

Let me begin by giving you a sense of what's going on in Congress concerning office automation. The issue is generally a new one for the Congress. When I joined his staff about a year ago, Representative George Miller, chairman of the Labor Standards Subcommittee, asked me to start looking at technology and automation and their effects on the workplace. The first thing you find is that in the early '60s there was a very similar sentiment to what you find today. The preamble to the Manpower Development Training Act passed in the '60s reads as if it were offered up as a bill in this most recent Congress to address the problems of dislocated workers.

In 1963 there was a national commission that did a complete study of automation, looking across industries and occupations in a matrix, taking each cell in the matrix and saying: "What's going to be the effect of technology on this occupation in this particular industry?"

I think we are beginning to see the start of that process again, though there is a certain amount of caution because of this earlier wave of concern. Our subcommittee has held one hearing on automation, on June 23, 1982, where we invited witnesses to talk about office and manufacturing automation. They started to lay out what they perceive to be the issues, what an agenda might be, and what the federal role might be. We plan to continue such hearings in the next Congress.

It is important to note that public policy on this issue is being formed not just in Education and Labor, but in a number of Congressional committees. The Science and Technology Committee has had hearings on robotics, on VDTs, and on the human factor in productivity. The Joint Economic Committee has issued a report on robotics, several reports on the semi-conductor industry, and on skill shortages related to micro-electronics. In the Senate there have also been several hearings on productivity and automation.

But these efforts have been single shots. There hasn't been a comprehensive look, and that's what our committee is beginning to offer. We plan to look at it systematically. To complement our work, our committee has commissioned two studies by the Office of Technology Assessment (OTA), which serves as technical advisor to Congress on technology. One is of the social effects of new manufacturing technology, the other on office technology. The manufacturing study is about six months in, and should be out in a year or so. The request just went in for the study of office automation. It will be reviewed shortly and will take about two years to complete.

These studies are not going to be definitive works, but they will serve to present a menu of issues that will become of national importance over the next 20 years. In addition, the reports will present options for Congressional response.

In the meantime, let me suggest some areas that one might look at or think about. These are things going on in Congress that certainly are going to affect automation. One immediate area, probably next year, could be a rewrite of the Vocational Education Act. The federal government has a small role in vocational education compared to the states, but in what direction should we being going with job training? In the clerical area, should we stop training people on typewriters and move only to word processors? How much is that going to cost? Should we train people as computer programmers? What if there is a glut in the market? So we will be discussing automation in the context of where education might go.

Related to that will be an effort, probably next year, to talk about science and math education. Generally this is talked about in terms of science and math education for people who are going to become computer scientists and engineers. But really there's a broader issue of technological literacy, of which computer literacy might be a sub-part. People from the Scandinavian countries have told me that if the workforce is not educated technologically, even at a minimum level, they are not going to be very good data stewards in the shop. A number of questions will come up. What level of science and math education are we going to have, and for whom? Should it be for adults or just school kids? If this bill is going to be for school children, what are we going to do about adult education? Education thus is another area to look at.

Another area of interest for Rep. Miller is in tax policies. What happens if you have an accelerated depreciation for new equipment, and you are cutting back on education funding? Are you really favoring capital substitution over labor? One witness at our hearing on June 23rd, someone in the business of selling automation equipment, suggested that we should tie the tax, the accelerated depreciation, to the requirement that any workers who are displaced be retrained. So that's one option.

In the retraining area there are a variety of options. One important question: who should pay for the retraining? If someone becomes unemployed because of automated equipment being brought into the company, some would argue that the company should internalize the cost and retrain them. But what about the person who has already been laid off because a plant somewhere else has been automated, which has lowered their labor costs and increased their market share. Whose responsibility is it to retrain them? And what about people who aren't in the labor force yet?

Then, of course, there are health and safety questions. A big issue: is it a state responsibility or a federal responsibility? It's not as simple as just considering this a federal responsibility. There are plenty of precedents where the states are the primary operators in their areas.

Another area is the design of equipment, the ergonomics issues. Does the federal government as an employer have a responsibility to its employees to assure that they have safe equipment? If the federal government set up particular standards for the procurement of equipment, would they in turn become ad hoc standards for that equipment across the entire economy? This is another interesting area.

Another area is direct federal government support for research and development. Should the military be directly funding automation for defense plants? What if it lowers the cost of producing weapon systems? Should we be funding basic research in artificial intelligence? Should we be funding basic research in robotics? What's the difference between basic science and technology? If we fund basic science and technological development, should our commitment to labor research be greater? Right now the Department of Labor is spending about $2 million this year on research on the effects of automation on employment. Is that too much or not enough?

At the moment these questions are rarely discussed. In the end many of these decisions will be made by Congress. You can influence their decisions.

Public Policy and the Employment Impacts of Office Computerization

Julyan Reid
Director of Communications
Ministry of State for Social Development
Government of Canada

By now there is general agreement that the introduction of "the chip" will indeed revolutionize the office and probably have far-reaching impacts on the whole structure of work in our economy. Most revolutions, unchecked, result in losers as well as winners. Women clerical and service workers have already been identified as the most likely losers. If our goal, collectively, is to shape this technological revolution so that everyone will benefit, then it is crucial to identify quickly what role each of the key participants can usefully play in that shaping process.

Government is only one of the players and public policy only one of the instruments of change. Unions, business, voluntary groups and academics also identify and act on the issues raised. Even within the context of public policy, orientations vary dramatically from country to country. In a tour of five European countries in late 1981, looking at research and public policy in the area of the impact of microprocessor technology on women and work, I found not only different levels of awareness but also different public policy approaches, both within Europe and between Europe and North America. A simplified analysis would show that public policy in North America focused on *industrial development* of the technology itself, and in Europe, particularly Scandinavia, public policy focused on *human resources* impact and development. The latter focus was not a recent reaction to a particular problem, but part of a long tradition of problem-solving with issues of technology and its impact on workers.

There are good reasons for different public policy reactions in different countries, which relate to history, culture, the role of government and other factors. For example, what type of government does the country have; is it socialist, capitalist, alternately one or the other? What kind of government intervention do the people tolerate? Is it a society that accepts a lot of regulation and legislation or do they tend to de-regulate and tell government: "Stay out of my backyard!"

Also, what is the traditional level of unionization, especially clerical unionization? What kind of control do the citizens and government have over their own economy, and therefore what kind of decisions can the policy-makers make in terms of reshaping the economy? And finally, what are the relevant cultural factors? What are the social assumptions that underlie their decisions? What is their attitude towards equality?

As a brief case study in the process of influencing public policy I will describe a situation in Canada in which a network of women worked to raise public and government awareness of the impact of microtechnology and its consequences for women, and sought ways to influence the decisions to be made.

Canada is like the United States in some ways: we have a low level of clerical unionization; a lower level of awareness of the impact of microtechnology on workers than in Europe; generally a capitalistic system, except that we have occasionally had socialist provincial governments. We are probably used to more intervention of government in our lives than Americans would likely tolerate. But, in comparison with the U.S., we have considerably less control over our own economy, and are sometimes described as a branch plant society. This makes us very vulnerable to decisions made elsewhere.

Within this context, we approach the issues of microtechnology in two ways; first on the level of economic development, such as industrial stimulation, and second in the area of social development, such as labor and health impacts, which to date is less developed than the first.

Governments, like business and individuals, plan ahead. They do planning and forecasting in the public policy domain in order to try to anticipate what the world is going to look like in the future, and plan accordingly. Within this planning context two questions can be posed: 1) Are the concerns of women, particularly in the area of labor displacement and equal opportunity, an integral part of that planning process? and 2) Do the day-to-day decisions of government take into account the scenarios for the future, or are the thinkers and planners in one box, and the decision-makers in another?

My feeling is that in North America we *plan* for industrial stimulation while we *react* to human problems.

When I started working on the issue of women and microtechnology, over two years ago, my immediate goal, both personal and professional, was relatively simple. It was to ensure that the interests of women, particularly the concerns raised by the impact of the new technology, would be an integral part of any policy and planning process in Canada, at least at the federal level.

At the time I was Director of Research for the Canadian Advisory Council on the Status of Women. It was clear to me, from the research and analysis being done in Europe, that the prognosis for women in the labor force was not good. By now you are all aware of the various reports and books: the Siemen's Report from Germany, the Nora-Minc report from France, Clive Jenkins' book in England predicting up to 30% unemployment, mainly in the office sector. At that time there seemed to be little or no awareness of any potential problem in the U.S. (with the notable exception of the 9to5 National Association of Working Women) and very little awareness in Canada, except among a small group of women in research, research management and unions. In Canada research work was being done, some of it in association with OECD in Paris, but it focused on economic development aspects: a) issues of productivity and rate of diffusion, and b) the development of high technology as a possible growth sector.

The first step that I and others took towards the goal of integration of the concerns of women was the identification of the problem. The way women's groups, women researchers and unions defined the issue was distinctly different from the way the more traditional economists, bureaucrats and businessmen defined it. The second step was to bring it to the attention of the public as well as to governments and businesses. This was done through research, publication of research and conferences. In Canada, Heather Menzies wrote **Women and the Chip** and **Computers on the Job**, and I asked Pat McDermott, who has written several articles on this subject in the **Canadian Forum**, to do a major research analysis for the Canadian Advisory Council on the Status of Women. Ratna Ray, Director of the Women's Bureau of Labour Canada, sponsored the first Canadian conference on the socio-economic impact of microtechnology, and asked several women speakers and representatives from women's groups to attend. Last June, four voluntary women's groups jointly sponsored a conference called "The Future is Now; Women and the Impact of Microtechnology," and drew hundreds of women in to speak and attend from a very wide variety of occupations and interests.

Through increasing awareness, publicity and general activity a more formal *public policy interest* has developed. In Canada we have had two official task forces. The report of the Labour Market Task Force (July, 1981) prepared for the Minister of Employment and Immigration projected that the contribution of the service sector employment to total employment growth will continue to fall in the 1980s, while the female share of the labor force is likely to rise, leading to a growing problem of unemployment among women. The report recommended increased efforts and special services (affirmative action) to ensure that women will be able to participate fully in the productive labor force.

Labour Canada sponsored a special Task Force on Microelectronics, headed by Dr. Margaret Fulton. The Task Force heard briefs from many women's groups, such as the National Action Committee on the Status of Women. The final report recommended that workers should not be required to use VDTs for more than five hours a day and that federal and provincial governments should set up health and safety regulations for workers who use VDTs and other automated office equipment. It also recommended that employers should pay for eye tests, pregnant workers should have the right to be reassigned without loss of benefits or seniority, government regulations should include standards for design of equipment in the workplace and that the Canada Labour Code, which affects the 10% of Canadian workers under federal jurisdiction, should be amended to make management-worker health and safety committees mandatory in offices employing more than 50 people. Task forces in themselves don't solve problems, but they bring the issues with specific recommendations one step closer to actual changes in regulations and policy actions.

Through the process of research, conferences, task forces, and other initiatives, the issues are being clarified, the public is becoming aware and specific recommendations are being made. The policy makers no longer dismiss women's concerns about the impact of microtechnology as irrelevant or of only marginal interest. Cabinet Ministers in Canada have made public statements of concern and the Minister of Employment and Immigration has made commitments to provide training and retraining courses. The *limited goal* is tentatively achieved. Virtually every discussion of microelectronics in government now mentions the impact on women.

Does this mean that we can expect any improvement in the situation of women in the near future? From where I sit now, in a central agency responsible for the overall management of social policy, I would be pessimistic. The labor displacement has come faster and harder than anyone predicted. The world economy is in difficulty, and for a country like Canada, so dependent on the economic health of other countries, the news is bad. We have an unemployment rate of 12% with projections of a continuing high rate. Although the recession is blamed, a lot of that job loss is hidden technological unemployment.

Companies are told and tell themselves that unless they become more productive, they will not survive. When machines replace people, productivity, as the economists measure it, is enhanced. A few years ago we all thought that the combination of a projected labor shortage in the '80s and increased oil revenues could spell a golden age of equality, prosperity and opportunity for women. The reality of today is somewhat different.

Now women face the danger of being told, as they have been told so often before, that if they only wait until the crisis is over, then their concerns will be addressed. All politicians and the bureaucrats who work to support the elected Ministers face competing priorities in their policy decision-making. Do they spend time and money on the ill-health of the economy? On the growing number of jobless? On pensions for old people? Where do the concerns of women workers fit in? Is it possible to lose even the small gains we've made? Have any of the solutions tried in other countries such as shorter hours, longer holidays, technological agreements really worked and could they work in Canada?

My fear is that when the economy recovers, women could find themselves less equal and more segregated than before. If that happens, then the questions I posed at the beginning on the involvement of the concerns of women in the planning process and the long-term effects of day-to-day decisions will have been answered in the negative. That doesn't have to happen and there is much that can be done, for example:

- When priorities compete, women simply have to compete harder. The short-term crises must never be allowed to displace the long-term goals of equality and a human workplace.
- There are many improvements to be made that are not expensive or competitive with other urgent policy goals, such as health and safety regulations, job and workplace design, greater public awareness and many others achievable in the short-term. This is the stuff of daily decision-making that builds up to long-term improvements.
- Governments respond to public pressure, especially articulate pressure. No one activity or recommendation will become a magic solution. We need to reshape traditional thinking about the nature of work and the rights of individuals, and the more activity that is generated in pursuit of these goals the better.

The employment impact of office computerization is above all a women's issue. If working women don't lead the way, no one else will.

Additional copies of this book may be ordered from the Working Women Education Fund for $12.95 plus $1.50 for postage and handling.

Also available from the Working Women Education Fund:

Race Against Time

What will the office of the future hold for office workers? This study explores the trends in office automation and its impact on the health, well-being, quality of work life and employment of women office workers. (1980)

$6.50 individuals $8.00 institutions

Warning: Health Hazards for Office Workers

From carcinogens in copying machines, to ventilation systems that circulate poisoned air, to an epidemic of stress-related diseases—health hazards facing office workers are a mounting concern. This report provides in-depth information on the dangers and offers solutions for a safe and healthful workplace. (1981)

$6.50 individuals $8.00 institutions

The Human Factor: 9 to 5's Consumer Guide to Word Processors

At least five million word processors are in use today. *The Human Factor* provides potential buyers and users with comparative information about safety and user-comfort features of automated office equipment. The guide was compiled by 9 to 5's Boston chapter. (1982)

$5.00

9 to 5: The Working Women's Guide to Office Survival

(New York: Penguin Books) Available October 1983.

Vital reading for employers and employees alike. A full length book packed with information confronting women office workers today: respect, pay, career mobility, health and safety, automation, child care, legal rights, and organizing. Managers will find the recommended employer policies particularly useful. $5.95

All orders must be sent prepaid. For all orders outside the U.S. please pay total in U.S. funds. Bulk rates are available on items ordered in quantity, and 9 to 5 members receive a discount on all publications; please write for more information and a complete publications list.

To Order: Add $1.50 for postage and handling for orders over $5.00.
Make check payable to Working Women Education Fund
1224 Huron Road, Cleveland, Ohio 44115.